ELVIS UNDERCOVER

BY

GAIL GIORGIO

ABOUT THE AUTHOR

Gail Giorgio is author of the *New York Times* bestseller *Is Elvis Alive?*—the opening round of her ongoing inquiry into the life of Elvis Presley and the circumstances surrounding his August 16, 1977, disappearance.

Gail wrote the television special *The Elvis Files* (featuring host Bill Bixby) and the sequel *The Elvis Conspiracy*, both among the highest-rated syndicated shows of the year; the documentary video *The Elvis Files* was also based on her works.

Among other accomplishments in this investigatory arena, Gail is the first person to document in entirety the famous series of post-"death" Elvis sightings in and around Kalamazoo, Michigan; she is also the first to provide public disclosure of a telephone conversation (recorded more than 11 years after Elvis's alleged death) with a person who identified himself as Elvis Presley.

Gail compiled the book *Roses to Elvis: Thoughts & Poems of Love From Fans of Elvis Presley*; she is author of the novel *Orion* and the book *Footprints in the Sand*.

Also among Gail's credits are magazine and newspaper articles (*Glamour, Guidepost, Atlanta Weekly, The Atlanta Journal*). Gail has been a talk-show host with WRNG Radio, she has worked in Oahu with the Hawaii Mission of the Methodist Church, and she has numerous credits in advertising, promotions, and musical video creations.

Library of Congress Catalog Number: 99-73368

ISBN 1-880092-49-2

Printed in Canada

First Edition

12 11 10 9 8 7 6 5 4 3 2 1

Bright Books
2729 Exposition Blvd. Suite 117
Austin, Texas 78703

CONTENTS

FOREWORD

The Presley Commission was formed during March and April of 1992 when it became evident to me that a thorough fact-finding mission was in order to determine the validity of prior information offered by Mrs. Giorgio and others. It was an important directive to provide the public interest with answers to questions that had become prevalent during previous investigations, and to protect the interests and privacy of Mr. Elvis Presley throughout our long search.

To this day documents relating to the matter of Elvis Presley's alleged death in 1977, as well as information in files currently held by the FBI, are still awaiting release nearly five years after initial requests under the guidelines of The Freedom of Information/Privacy Act. The controversy surrounding this case must end. The public interest must be satisfied. I congratulate Gail Giorgio for her continued efforts on behalf of matters concerning this case and providing such a positive outlook.

In the final analysis, if our information serves us correctly, Mr. Presley must be able to provide us with his version of what happened in August 1977. Only then can we fully understand the real tragedy, not of a man who passed away, but of the consequences based on the events of that day and surrounding time. Only then can this great historical controversy truly find its resting place.

Philip W. Aitcheson
National Director (Ret.)
Executive Liaison Consultant

***

For information regarding The Presley Commission's work, including its publication *The Presley Report*, please contact:

The Presley Commission
P.O. Box 602
Moneta, VA 24121-0602

DEDICATION

A very special thanks to the late Mae Axton, co-author of the song "Heartbreak Hotel," Phillip Aitcheson, former director of the Presley Commission, attorney Tom Austin, the Baums: Cindy, Jay and Murray, Maria Columbus, David Dortort, Frank and Marie D'Orio, agent/editor Jamie Forbes, Larry Geller, agent/publisher Jeff Herman, publisher Bill Hanson, design editor Kristal McManigal, M. Slayton, Elvis' first cousin Gene Smith, handwriting expert Paul Weast, law enforcement experts B. and D. Wines, members of *The Gathering* and *The Sharing*, with particular thanks to Edie Bippus, Elna Davis, Lynn Free, Jon Hamel, Terrina Rush, Louise Welling, and a host of "other eyes and ears." Also, an endearing thanks to Luc Dionne (my co-author on the future book *Operation Fountain Pen*,) and especially office assistants Maria Giorgio and Amy Wightman Giorgio, whose help has been invaluable.

Last, but hardly least, my family: Carm, Maria, Jim, Chris, Amy, Noel, Sheila, Tasha, C.J., Mom & Dad G., and my dear Aunt Mim.

And, of course, to the man himself: Elvis Aron Presley.

We are truly "Souls having a human experience." I'm so happy you're a part of mine!

PREFACE

Is Elvis Presley alive? Yes, this is a strong question, one that has proved extremely volatile and has pitched me into the middle of the type of controversy one usually associates with conspiracies and cover-ups on the scale of high-level international espionage or assassination plots. However, my ongoing investigation has convinced me—through an overwhelming wealth of documentary and anecdotal evidence that continues to accumulate—that it is very possible Elvis Presley did not die on August 16, 1977. And, further, I am persuaded Elvis Presley might make a public reappearance, and his return may well occur in the not-too-distant future.

This question and answer have more significance when one considers that, at the end of May 1999, the recently produced movie *Finding Graceland* was shown on Cinemax.

One of the executive producers is Priscilla Presley.

The film, produced by Avenue Pictures and distributed by Largo Entertainment in Los Angeles, had the full cooperation of Elvis Presley Enterprises, with key scenes shot inside Graceland and around Memphis.

The premise of the film is that Elvis Presley is alive, that he faked his death over twenty years ago, and that he is intent on returning to Graceland and making a comeback.

Elvis (played by Harvey Keitel) hitches a ride with a young widower named Bryon (played by Johnathan Schaech) whom Elvis nicknames "Byrn." Byrn has recently lost his wife in a car/train accident in Memphis and has nothing to live for. He still drives the battered '59 Cadillac convertible in which his wife was killed. (There are more than a few close shots of the Caddy's license tag #56-0367, which intrigued me because of Elvis's interest in numerology. However, if there is a hidden meaning in this combination of numbers, only Elvis knows what it is.)

Elvis is smitten with the '59 Caddy, knows its history, then convinces Byrn to take him to Memphis, that he [Elvis] has to get there by "Sunday noon." Elvis admits he has turned sixty awhile back, that he had faked his death (saying, "August 16th is the day I died"), etc. Byrn does not believe this seemingly down-and-out drifter is Elvis Presley, but rather an impersonator.

A series of events, little by little, eventually causes Byrn to wonder *if* there is something to this man's story, one event being when the two of them are stopped by a Sheriff Haynes, whom Elvis recognizes as a childhood friend from East Tupelo. At first Sheriff Haynes does not believe Elvis is alive or in fact it is Elvis he has stopped. However, when Elvis relates childhood events (the sharing of poetry in the fifth grade, a fall that Haynes caused upon Elvis, Haynes' nickname of "Hef" and the fact that Hef called Elvis "Hiss" as a child), the sheriff then *knows* it is really Elvis and that he is indeed alive. Elvis asks Hef to forgive his "abrupt farewell."

Byrn is stymied.

Elvis is also able to answer "Elvis" questions Byrn poses: his shoe size, when he purchased Graceland, Army ID numbers, etc. Still, Byrn is skeptical.

While they are on the road together, Elvis has nightmares about "his wife and child."

The advice that Elvis imparts to the young man is sprinkled with personal revelations such as:

- I lost sight of what was me.
- One day my life spiraled out of my hands.
- I lost sight of what was meaningful—my wife, my child, my music.
- I found that I needed time just to catch my breath, so I split.
- I travel around lending "hep" to folks who need it.
- Sometimes a man has to give up what's dearest to him to find peace.
- There is no such thing as coincidence.
- I fix what I break.

- I'm rich, famous, vulnerable.
- The best gratuity is friendship.
- If money meant that much to me, I wouldn't have left the mansion behind.
- You have to forgive.
- Have faith that the next load you know won't cause you so much pain.
- The life I left wasn't so bad after all.

There is a background song with the lyrics of "a wayward soul coming home..." Other songs such as "Walking in Memphis," and one about seeing the ghost of Elvis, play in the background. (Not sung by Elvis.)

Dialogue and feelings suggest that Elvis is trying to "see the true heart of people" by acting "down and out," yet at one point it becomes clear that this drifter is actually well-to-do when he secretly has Byrn's Caddy restored to mint condition, a gift to the young man who has befriended him and lent him a helping hand.

During their travels they meet a young woman named Ashley (played by Bridget Fonda), who tells Byrn that everyone needs guidance. What difference does it make if you get it from Jesus, Buddha or Elvis?

Elvis admits that when his mama died, he wanted to jump in the grave with her, that he thought he'd never trust a woman—until he met Priscilla. There is a scene where Elvis (pretending to be an impersonator) gets stage sickness right before performing (just like Elvis did). Byrn finds an article in Elvis's wallet about August 16th, *and* the death of the family of a man named Jon Burrows. When Byrn questions Elvis about this, Elvis says he had the article made up ages ago because some folks need "me to have a more believable identity." (Jon Burrows is the code name Elvis used in his 1970 letter to President Nixon, reproduced in this book.)

Thinking that perhaps Elvis is this man named Burrows, Ashley volunteers to do a search, but finds no such family listed in the Memphis area.

Elvis wears a lightning bolt around his neck, and a diamond horseshoe ring.

They head to Memphis with Elvis telling Byrn that this is not "the first time I've tried coming home." Once inside Graceland it is apparent Elvis knows his way around. A poignant scene occurs when Elvis drops to the hallway stairs and sobs, "There's nobody here..."

At one point in the movie, Elvis says, "You'll be sorry once I'm gone."

The movie nears its end with a candlelight vigil of the anniversary of Elvis's death. The enormity of the crowds makes Elvis realize, "that to them *I am home.*" He shouts to the crowd to "Remember the king..."

Seeing that Byrn is on the mend (a romance is blossoming between Byrn and Ashley), he tells Byrn that he is going to travel again, maybe hitch a train ride. He also says, "It's never too late for a comeback."

The movie ends with two songs sung by Elvis, one being "If I Can Dream," and then Elvis hopping a train boxcar. Something strange occurs: On the boxcar is a bum whom Elvis greets. The camera closes in on the bum, closer and closer.

Why is this strange? Because it may be the *real* Elvis as the bum!

Why do I question this? I was once told a story by a friend/relative of Elvis Presley. "If you want to know the heart of people you have to be one of the crowd," he said. Thus, in order to sometimes test the heart of people, Elvis was known to don disguises, one being that of a bum. (By the way, the bum is alone in each frame, thus *if* it is Elvis-in-disguise, he could have been filmed by himself with no other actors around.)

Should *Finding Graceland* be rerun on Cinemax, video it and do a pause/still on the bum. Tell me what you think.

As an aside I noted at least one of Elvis's friends in the movie, especially the casino scenes. I recall that back in 1988 this friend blasted me on the radio for asking if Elvis could be alive. Approximately ten years later he's a paid extra in a film whose premise is that Elvis *is* alive and may make a comeback! The fact that this film has Priscilla Presley as one of its executive producers should not go unnoticed, nor the fact that this film was in conjunction (with permission) of Elvis Presley Enterprises.

They, by their own hand, are giving credibility to my earlier question: Is Elvis alive? And is he coming back?

The media is quick to pick up on the sensational aspects of this case, which are indeed exciting and provocative. The blessing of public exposure has, thankfully, fueled the discussion and kept me hard at work to uncover previously shrouded mysteries.

- There has long been widespread speculation among family and friends, as well as independent observers, that the body viewed by the public at Graceland prior to the funeral was not that of Elvis Presley—and was perhaps not a real body at all.
- Among the many reported Elvis sightings (some of them undoubtedly frivolous) are a group that stand up under the harsh light of investigative scrutiny.
- Elvis Presley's handwriting appears on at least two official documents (in an FBI file and a medical-examiner's report) executed after the August 16, 1977, date of Elvis Presley's alleged death. Obviously, the existence of even a single piece of evidence such as this means that Elvis did not die—at least not under circumstances anything like those which have been publicly asserted.

I have spoken with a man who claimed to be Elvis Presley, and all clues dropped during our talk corroborate this identity. (A complete transcription of the telephone call in question is included in Chapter 9.) Even after our discussion, the whens and whys of Elvis's return are an open question. Hints are that Elvis's return ties in with a personal mission to help humanity—though there is speculation of more personal motivation. And there are those who believe his return is imminent, though, as Elvis himself has written: "Should I return, you would not recognize me."

Why Elvis chose to disappear, and thus hoaxed his own death, is central to one of the most compelling parts of this scenario:

Operation Fountain Pen, the FBI's dangerous undercover investigation of an international crime syndicate in which Elvis Presley, as a certified government agent-at-large, played a crucial and hazardous role.

While important, the more publicized elements of this controversy are only the glittering edge of a story that to a great extent has remained buried—until now. You may believe that Elvis's disappearance, rather than death, is clear, based on the materials in this book—or you may choose not to believe this account at all.

I am convinced that a look at the results of my research, if it pertained to anyone else but Elvis Presley, would shock most people into stating readily: "Of course he's alive." But we're talking about Elvis Presley—an American hero and a billion-dollar industry. The authorized version of the circumstances surrounding August 16, 1977, at Graceland has commanded the kind of official support that would view all talk of plots, cover-ups, and sightings—however convincing—as no more than an entertaining pastime.

I assure you this is not the case.

Please read on, examine the evidence at hand, and consider the many questions raised by both circumstance and documented events—and then make up your own mind.

Dead or alive, Elvis Presley is an American treasure and for me will always inspire my personal search.

INTRODUCTION

"What book about Elvis Presley did Tudor Publishing receive 1 to 1 ¹/₂ million orders for during its first three weeks on the market?"

This was one of the questions asked in the 1990s version of the game The New Trivial Pursuit. On the reverse side of the game card is the answer: *Is Elvis Alive?*

I stared at the game card and shook my head. Never in a zillion years would I have guessed that a book I had written would actually spark such controversy as to become a part of the popular culture.

Is Elvis alive? It seemed a rather logical question to have asked back in 1977, considering the mystery and contradictions surrounding the widely reported death of the most popular entertainer of this century. It was a question also asked in various ways by the thousands of fans who had filed past Elvis Presley's open coffin on August 17, 1977:

"That doesn't look like Elvis."

"He looks too young."

"Where did that pug nose come from?"

"Why are there no scars on his hands? Elvis had scars on his hands from karate."

And the most constantly heard remark:

"Why are there beads of sweat on the body? Dead bodies don't sweat, do they?"

This same observation was also made by at least one family member. Several years after Elvis's death, I spoke on the telephone with Gene Smith, Elvis's first cousin (Gene's mother, Lavalle, and Elvis's mother, Gladys, were sisters). Later Gene and I met when we were filming the documentary video *The Elvis Files.*

Born seven weeks before Elvis, Gene grew up with his illustrious cousin, first in Tupelo, Mississippi, where they played together and double-dated, and later in Memphis, Tennessee, where they worked together at Precision Tools.

"We were closer than brothers," Gene told me. "Aunt Gladys always wanted me to stay around Elvis, especially when he slept. I'd go out on the road with him, and sleep in the same room because Elvis walked in his sleep—we were always afraid he'd walk out of a window or something. I could sleep in a way that the slightest sound woke me. I worked for Elvis well into the sixties, but we always stayed close. It's strange, all these books written about Elvis, about his growing up, what he did, what we did..."

Gene paused thoughtfully. "Those people who wrote about Elvis's growing-up years didn't even know him back then. I knew what went on because I was there. I loved Aunt Gladys like a mother. Someday I think I should write a book..."

(**AUTHOR'S NOTE**: Gene recently wrote his book, titled *Elvis's Man Friday*, published by Light of Day in Nashville, Tennessee.)

I finally met Gene in June of 1990 while on location in the Los Angeles area filming a documentary in which Gene was a guest. I appreciated his warmth and realness. Gene has the blue eyes with that Presley twinkle, as well as a keen sense of humor. Gene reiterated what he had told me earlier on the telephone. "I saw Elvis a few weeks before August 16th," he said. "Elvis told me, 'Gene, I envy you. You can go anywhere you want to. If you want to stop someplace for a beer, you can. I'm living the most miserable son-of-a-bitchin' life anyone could live!' Elvis also told me that shortly before the 16th he would be going away for a while, but that he would contact me later."

When Gene heard Elvis had died, he said he couldn't believe it, that he felt something was wrong, and then knew something was wrong when he went to the viewing. "The first thing I saw when I went to the coffin," Gene related, "was the hands. They weren't Elvis's. You see, Elvis's hands were big and beat up, calluses on the knuckles, scars, a crooked finger, all this from karate, breaking boards, smashing bricks. The hands in the coffin were small and as smooth as a woman's, smooth as a baby's behind. They were definitely not Elvis's hands. Plus, the sideburns were glued on; one was sticking straight out at the side. When I noticed this, some man came over and patted it back down, like he was sticking it back on. The nose was all wrong, pugged. Elvis had a straight nose. The eyebrows were wrong, the forehead wrong, hairline wrong. I could even see where the hair had been glued on around the forehead. You could see the glue."

"Could it have been a wax dummy?" I asked Gene.

"Could have been," Gene responded. "I thought it was."

"Many who viewed the body in the coffin noted what they termed as 'beads of sweat,'" I told him.

"That's true," Gene answered. "I saw it, too."

Laughingly, I reminded Gene that dead bodies don't sweat. He said, "I know. Plus," he added, "if it was a wax dummy, then there had to have been an air-conditioner in the coffin. I think there might have been. I was one of the pallbearers, and that coffin was so heavy I fell to my knees. The coffin was too heavy to have had just a body in it."

My impression at that time was that Gene was not a part of any death-hoax plot in its initial planning stage. However, my instincts told me he knew more than he was saying, especially after spending time with him in Los Angeles when Gene said he thought Elvis liked me because I had "Gladys's eyes." This became clearer to me and to many fans after they read Gene's book *Elvis's Man Friday*. Basically, to paraphrase Gene Smith, at the end of his book Gene concludes by saying that the account he has given of Elvis's life has no ending because only Sivle Yelserp can tell us how it will be concluded. He then basically says this will eventually happen.

Sivle Yelserp is Elvis Presley spelled backward. Other family members have told me Sivle Yelserp was a code name often used to "get through to Elvis at Graceland."

Further proof that Gene may either think or know that Elvis is alive occurs in the acknowledgments to his book, where he gives a special thanks to "Sivle Yelserp."

Seeing and reading this with my own eyes, I wondered if other family members or friends knew more than they said. Again I saw my question had grounds when, at the end of 1996, Billy Smith, another Elvis cousin as well as one of Elvis's closest friends, would admit to a London newspaper a shocking revelation: Elvis Presley had not died on August 16, 1977.

Billy's interview in conjunction with another close Elvis friend, Marty Lacker, will be fully discussed later in this book. It's intriguing to say the least.

"Is Elvis alive?" thus became a question that became the "shot heard 'round the world."

"Is Elvis alive?" also became a question that would rock the world by sending a ripple of shock waves from one corner of the planet to the other, the first shock wave being, "Elvis is dead"—the second shock wave being, "But, is he...?"

Publicly I had fired the first shot. Publicly I had caused the first of a series of shock waves that would eventually lead me from Graceland to the White House.

Ironically, Graceland is the second-most-visited house in the United States, the first being the White House, home of the President of the United States. I say "ironically" because of Elvis Presley's White House connections, the telephone calls he made from Graceland to the President of the United States, and the calls made from the President to Elvis Presley shortly before Elvis's death.

What did these calls concern?

These would be the sort of questions that needed answering. I needed to know why, after speaking with Elvis Presley, the President of the United States, James Earl ("Jimmy") Carter, then spoke with the administrator of the Drug Enforcement Administration (DEA). This question became more significant when I considered that Elvis Presley had seven years earlier been appointed a special agent with the DEA by another U.S. President, Richard Nixon.

On the private level, asking if Elvis might be alive had turned my life upside down and inside out. Had I known that by asking this question I would be crucified by many in the media, that I would be living proof of the proverbial "let's kill the messenger who brings the news," I doubt I would have continued forward.

Had I known that by asking this question I was walking on sacred ground where even angels feared to tread, I would have raced backward at a speed that would break Olympic records.

Like David standing in the shadow of a mighty Goliath, I was standing in the shadows of a giant icon known as Elvis Aron Presley. In the twenty years since I first publicly posed the "Is Elvis alive?" question, the Elvis "power-machine" has become a Goliath of unfathomable size.

The appointment of Elvis Presley as agent-at-large by President Nixon took on greater significance when I recalled a strange telephone call received by one of my book publicists after I had

appeared on a radio talk show regarding my book *Is Elvis Alive?*
"Tell Gail," the mystery voice stated, "that the matter concerning
the cover-up [of Elvis Presley's alleged death] is more far reaching
and involves more power and money than she even realizes. What
she's discovered is only the tip of the iceberg…"

Only the tip of the iceberg…?

This entire matter was already beginning to sound like a bad
movie. Still, did this "tip of the iceberg" have anything to do with a
theory casually posed in my book? I quote: "Another theory, this
one from a newspaper friend, is that since Elvis was a Special Agent
of the Bureau of Narcotics and Dangerous Drugs, he is working
undercover as an agent, and that our government provided him
with new credentials, even helped orchestrate a cover-up."

Had I unwittingly stumbled onto a "Musical Watergate"?

Was the mystery caller my "Deep Throat"?

The more questions I asked, the more new questions were
posed, and the more convinced I became that I had indeed
stumbled onto a Musical Watergate. The mystery caller's words—
"…more far reaching and involves more power and money than she
even realizes"—came back to haunt me many times and in many
ways. One of the most stunning of the revelations to come was
hinted at in the November 2, 1992, letter received by Maria
Columbus, president of the Elvis Special Fan Club, from the
Department of the Treasury, Bureau of Alcohol, Tobacco and
Firearms in Washington, D.C.

This letter states the following: "During the period of 1974
through 1976, Mr. Presley provided one of our undercover agents,
who was a musician, a job cover. Mr. Presley confirmed to anyone
inquiring that the agent/musician was a member of one of his
traveling bands. Although Mr. Presley was not actively involved in
any of the investigations, his assistance in this regard made it
possible for our agent to develop a number of quality investigations."

What kind of investigation would have necessitated Elvis to lie?
Why was he giving cover to an undercover agent in the first place?
What was going on?

And lastly, if Elvis Presley lied about this agent's presence in his band, a lie condoned by the government and perhaps even orchestrated by the government, was it possible that this same government might lie about Elvis's true involvement in this covert operation, especially if it put either the agent's or Mr. Presley's life at risk?

Was it feasible that the government of the United States of America ever lied, valid reasons or not, to its people?

Is it possible that the answer to this question rests in the question itself?

It was then I decided to obtain copies of all Federal Bureau of Investigation files on Elvis Presley. They were provided to me in 1989. During my perusal of these files I discovered an FBI case involving an FBI undercover operative called Operation Fountain Pen, a file not declassified until 1985, almost eight years after Elvis Presley's death.

The next obvious question: Why was this file kept secret for so many years? More importantly and most shockingly: Why are 624 pages of this file still classified "top security" with 74 of them for "national security" or "foreign policy" reasons?

What is it that we're not allowed to know about Elvis Presley? And why would this knowledge be detrimental to the security of our nation?

Should I dare try to determine what might be hidden beneath the "tip of the iceberg"?

I put these new questions to the ultimate test.

The results are mind-boggling.

PROLOGUE

To get a feel for what may have been happening shortly before the disappearance of Elvis Presley, perhaps the reader could imagine something like the following as the opening scene to a film:

Opening scene pre-credits/full color:
At the height of a massive winding staircase stands a **Man** in his early forties.

Camera pauses.
Man is wearing a dark navy jacket that is partially unzipped. Three gold letters are monogrammed on jacket:

Camera close on monogrammed letters: "DEA."
Beneath jacket **Man** wears a denim shirt. Black leather boots peer from beneath newly pressed jeans. **Man**'s dark hair displays graying sideburns, and his crystal-blue eyes appear to be agonizing over something. He looks down, sighs deeply, then slowly, step by step, descends. An involuntary shudder vibrates through him, and he grabs the banister for support.

Camera close on expensive diamond ring on his right-hand ring finger.
The only sound heard is the click of his boot-heel as it meets with the white marble floor of the center hall of his mansion.

Camera pulls back, full shot of Man:
Again, **Man** pauses. Incredible pain distorts chiseled features. He turns toward the left where in the living room **Two Men** in navy-blue suits, white shirts, and red-white-and-blue-striped ties sit waiting. Middle-aged, their expressions are serious. The **Two Men** rise slowly, then carefully make their approach. **One Man** flashes a badge.
"Mr. Presley?" the shorter of the two asks.

The **Man** in the monogrammed jacket nods cautiously.
"We're with the FBI…"

Cut to:
Credits continue to roll as **Camera** pans **Graceland**, follows shrubbed pathway to back building that houses the office of **Vernon Presley**:
Pause in Credits:

Cut to:
1976—Memphis, Tennessee
Elvis Presley is with his father, **Vernon Presley,** in **Vernon's** private office. **Vernon** sits behind a desk while **Elvis** paces back and forth. **Elvis** is wearing the same outfit as when meeting with agents from the FBI.

"Did you get hold of Nigel Winfield?" **Elvis** asks.

Vernon nods.

"Did you tell him that we need money bad?"

Vernon sighs. "Yeah. He was surprised, what with all the money you make. I told him that you've been having money problems— bad investments, expensive gifts, and those damn payroll costs, which is the truth. You gotta let some of those guys go, son…"

"Okay, Daddy. I know. We'll deal with that later. Is Nigel going to help us find a buyer for the JetStar, yes or no?"

"He'd have a better chance of getting a good price for the *Lisa Marie*. It's got the TCB and gold lightning bolt on its tail section. Everyone knows that plane is yours. Winfield got it for you for a little over a million. I wouldn't be surprised if he could get three million for it, maybe more."

"No. That'd be like selling my little girl. That'd be a bad omen. Can't do it, Daddy. Plus, I spent close to a million remodeling."

"You know the JetStar's gonna have to be updated."

Elvis whirls around. "Tell Winfield to find us a buyer for the JetStar, and only the JetStar. Time is closing in—if we're gonna meet the August 16, 1977 date. It's got to be that date—2001—that's the lucky number. Get hold of Beecher Smith at his law office—tell him what's going down…"

Cut to:
Credits resume, ending with a black-and-white flashback in time: 1970 B&W shots of **President Richard Nixon**'s appointment of **Elvis Presley** as a federal agent-at-large with the DEA.
End of opening scene.

***

1

AGENT PRESLEY

In order to appreciate how and why Elvis Presley became involved in Operation Fountain Pen—one of the most dangerous FBI undercover operations ever launched—it is essential to emphasize that the same Elvis Presley who was a world-renowned entertainer was also a bona fide agent-at-large with the DEA. There can be no doubt that Elvis Presley had the character required to keep his involvement with this heavily classified government operation a top secret.

Once you understand how deeply Elvis felt about serving America, how deeply spiritual he was, and the depth of his patriotism, you'll understand this truth: Elvis Presley put his life on the line for this country, and in doing so may have been forced to "die."

Further, even if originally posed via books and television specials that I wrote—*Is Elvis Alive?* and *The Elvis Files*—it is equally important to repeat the clues that Elvis Presley may have left behind that declared, "I did not die on August 16, 1977."

Equally important to realize is that, despite Elvis's being a collector of law-enforcement badges, his appointment by President Richard Nixon as a special agent with the DEA was a bona fide appointment, not a token publicity move. Witnessing this historic meeting on December 21, 1970, were Jerry Schilling and Sonny West. Not only did these men work for Elvis, they were close friends as well. A White House photographer snapped over two dozen pictures of this event and, although all the details of the

Nixon–Presley meeting are not known, the National Archives and Records Administration has over 40 million pages of documents pertaining to the Nixon Administration. Included are documents regarding Elvis's visit to the Oval Office.

What prompted Elvis to offer his services to our nation?

Both Elvis and President Nixon called drugs "America's number-one problem." By 1970 Nixon had launched a national crusade against drugs, which fired up Elvis, especially when he learned that the President was planning to set up a powerful drug-enforcement agency that was to be modeled after the FBI and CIA. Nixon thought this new agency could become one of the most powerful arms of our government.

When Elvis decided to do something it was usually based upon the premise, "It's now or never." Elvis simply left Graceland late one night in December of 1970, and with friend Jerry Schilling (Sonny West was to catch a later flight) caught the red-eye special to Washington with the hope of seeing someone in power, perhaps the head of the Bureau of Narcotics and Dangerous Drugs or even a meeting with J. Edgar Hoover, the legendary figure who was then head of the Federal Bureau of Investigation.

Elvis told no one at Graceland where he was going—or, in fact, that he was going. While in Washington he thought he would try to see the President of the United States as well. He had no appointment, but—well, he was Elvis Presley. On the same flight as Elvis was California Senator George Murphy. After Elvis explained to the senator his need to serve in the war against drugs, the senator promised he would make an appointment for Elvis the following morning with John Ingersoll, the director of the Bureau of Narcotics and Dangerous Drugs (BNDD); the senator as well promised to call the offices of the FBI.

Elvis decided he personally would be the one to try to arrange a meeting with President Nixon. Elvis wanted to offer the President his weight as an entertainer. After all, he could speak to a range of people that few others could. During the American Airlines flight Elvis wrote his six-page letter to President Nixon:

Elvis Presley's Letter
to
President Richard Nixon
December 1970

Dear Mr. President,

First I would like to introduce myself. I am Elvis Presley and admire you and have great respect for your office. I talked to Vice President Agnew in Palm Spring 3 weeks ago and expressed my concern for our country. The Drug Culture, the Hippie Elements, the SDS, Black Panthers, etc. do not consider me as their enemy or as they call it The Establishment. I call it America and I love it. Sir, I can and will be of any service that I can to help the country out. I have no concern or motives other than helping the country out. So I wish not to be given a title or an appointed position. I can and will do more good if I were made a Federal Agent at Large, and I will help out by doing it my way through my communication with people of all ages. First and foremost I am an entertainer but all I need is the Federal credentials. I am on this plane with Senator George Murphy and we have been discussing the problems that our country is faced with. So I am staying at the Washington Hotel, Room 505-506-507—I have two men who work with me by the name of Jerry Schilling and Sonny West. I am registered under the name of Jon Burrows. I will be here for as long as it takes to get the credentials of a Federal Agent. I have done an in-depth study of drug abuse and communistic brainwashing techniques and I am right in the middle of this whole thing where I can and will do the most good. I am glad to help just so long as it is kept very private. You can have your staff or whomever call me anytime today, tonight or tomorrow. I was nominated this coming year one of America's Ten Most Outstanding Young Men. That will be in January 18 in my home town of Memphis,

Tenn. I am sending you the short autobiography about myself so you can better understand my approach. I would love to meet you just to say hello if you're not too busy.

Respectfully,
Elvis Presley

P.S. I believe that you, Sir, were one of the Top Ten Outstanding Men of America. I have a personal gift for you also which I would like to present to you and you can accept it or I will keep it for you until you can take it.

The last page of this letter contains personal telephone numbers where Elvis could be reached either in Beverly Hills, Palm Springs, or Memphis. As soon as Elvis and Jerry arrived in Washington, he and Jerry drove to the gates of the White House. Elvis introduced himself to the guard, handed the guard his letter to the President, then drove to the Washington Hotel and checked in. At this point Jerry convinced Elvis that Graceland had to be notified of Elvis's whereabouts. Elvis's friend and bodyguard, Sonny West, was summoned to Washington. The next day Elvis drove to the Justice Building and met with the deputy director of the drug agency, John Finlator, where Elvis was told that only bona fide agents of the bureau could be issued badges. This is important to keep in mind because of the various rumors and suppositions to the effect that Elvis's eventual appointment was only "a token one."

When Elvis returned to the Washington Hotel, Jerry Schilling told him the President had called and would see Elvis. Nixon's right-hand man in the war against drugs was Egil (Bud) Krogh. At the White House Krogh met Presley, Schilling, and West (who had just arrived in Washington) and, after telling Schilling and West they would have to wait elsewhere due to security, Elvis was ushered into the Oval Office. After some small talk, Elvis explained to President Nixon his purpose in being there, how he wished to serve the nation, his dedication to the country, and how he could gather information secretly, as people told him things they would never tell others.

President Nixon was so impressed with Elvis's commitment that he gave the orders to have a BNDD badge (BNDD stands for Bureau of Narcotics and Dangerous Drugs, which was later named the Drug Enforcement Administration [DEA]) as well as a complete set of credentials prepared immediately for Elvis Presley. Afterward, Elvis asked if his aides, Schilling and West, could be part of the picture-taking ceremony in the President's Oval Office. President Nixon agreed.

In the December 21, 1970, White House memo sent to H.R. Haldeman from presidential assistant Dwight L. Chapin, it was determined that Presley was important enough not to be "pushed off on the Vice President" and everyone agreed it would be a good idea for Elvis Presley to become a "Federal agent at large." In this memorandum Chapin stressed: "Presley was voted one of the ten outstanding young men for next year and this was based upon his work in the field of drugs."

Elvis received his commendation as one of the ten outstanding young men on January 18, 1971, in Memphis. Notably, another soon-to-be U.S. President presented this award to Elvis—George Bush. Again, because of Elvis's desire to do things "his way" and to do them secretly, we do not know how much or how often or what exactly it was that Elvis did in the field of drugs to earn this nomination. What the above-mentioned memo illustrates is that by 1970 Elvis was already serving his country and his government in one way or another. It is interesting to note that Elvis told President Nixon that he had been "studying the drug culture for over ten years." Elvis also indicated that he could get into any cultural group easily and be "accepted."

According to Krogh: "The President mentioned that he thought Presley could reach young people, and that it was important for Presley to retain his credibility. Presley responded that he did his thing by 'just singing.' He said that he could not get to the kids if he made a speech on the stage. The President nodded in agreement."

Krogh, in another interesting memo, noted: "Presley indicated to the President in a very emotional manner that he was 'on your side.' Presley kept repeating that he wanted to be helpful, that he wanted to restore some respect for the flag which was being lost. He mentioned that he was just a poor boy from Tennessee who had gotten a lot from his country, which in some way he wanted to repay. At the conclusion of the meeting, Presley again told the President how much he supported him, and then, in a surprising, spontaneous gesture, put his left arm around the President and hugged him."

There is little doubt not only that Presley was sincere in his offerings but also that this appointment was real—real enough that, two years later, famed *Washington Post* columnist Jack Anderson began his January 27, 1972, article with the headline: PRESLEY GETS NARCOTICS BUREAU BADGE. According to Anderson's article, Deputy Narcotics Director John Finlator sought to enlist Presley in the antidrug fight. "Finlator invited the singer to the Narcotics Bureau for a quiet visit and arranged for the guards to admit him under the pseudonym 'John Burroughs.' When Finlator finally handed Presley the badge and promised to issue him consultant credentials, the singer was overcome with emotion, and his eyes became misty."

A January 27, 1972, memo from Bud Krogh regarding Anderson's column in the *Post* supported Presley's desire and determination to fight drugs. Although Anderson wrote about Presley's appointment, it's interesting to note that Elvis had managed to keep a low profile for over two years.

There is no doubt that Elvis Presley was a federal agent with the DEA. "By Presidential dictum," Jack Anderson wrote in the *Washington Post*, "Elvis Presley, the swivel hipped singer, has been issued a federal narcotics badge."

***

For a full set of the Richard Nixon-Elvis Presley White House pictures, contact:

Richard E. McNeill
Archives Specialist
Nixon Presidential Materials
National Archives & Records
Washington, DC 20408

2

THE LAW ENFORCER

It is certain that Elvis's romance with law and order ran deep—despite the attitudes often displayed to the public through Elvis's onstage image. In his heart Elvis was a dedicated American. This dedication expanded into areas beyond the DEA. Still, it was this federal appointment that Elvis was the most proud of—an appointment that would possibly, eventually, change his entire life. The truth is that, because of who he was, Elvis Presley could get to the kind of people and places others could not. "The most effective agent," Elvis was heard to say, "is the one least suspected, one who has another job…" In Elvis's case, his "other job" was that of an entertainer. Who would suspect Elvis Presley of working undercover?

Although we don't know exactly how far back Elvis's work in law enforcement went, records attest that from 1970 to 1977 Elvis Presley was connected to two U.S. Presidents, both of whom wanted his services to help them and the country in the war against drugs. In a letter dated November 29, 1982, from Bob Pritchett, of the Department of the Treasury, to Maria Columbus, president of the Elvis Special Fan Club, we are told that during the years 1974, 1975, and 1976, "Mr. Presley provided one of our undercover agents, who was a musician, a job cover." Essentially what this means is that for several years an undercover agent was being provided cover by Elvis Presley, himself an agent. Like Elvis, this agent also had "another job," which makes detection less likely and the assignment less dangerous.

It is clear from the government's correspondence with Maria Columbus that the undercover agent's identity had to be kept a secret. It is interesting to note in a second, December 22, 1982, letter to Maria Columbus from Pritchett, that the "files are Criminal Investigative files." Translated, this means a criminal investigation was taking place over approximately a three-year period and that Elvis was at least involved to the point of "providing cover" for another federal agent. It's highly probable that Elvis may have been involved in this criminal investigation to a far greater degree than we know, especially when one takes into consideration the possible extent of Elvis's role in Operation Fountain Pen, which was without doubt one of the most dangerous undercover operatives ever undertaken by the FBI.

(In that same December 22, 1982, letter from Pritchett to Columbus he insists "our undercover agent does not want his name made known to the public.")

Here another question arises. Given that Elvis Presley was a federal agent-at-large with the DEA and was at least involved in providing cover to another agent for three years, we may further take into account Elvis's ongoing associations with at least two U.S. Presidents, President Nixon and President Carter, both of whom he spoke with shortly before August 16, 1977. Now we ask: Is it possible that Elvis in turn became the target of drug dealers who were the focus of the criminal investigations of 1974 to 1976?

As an aside, although Jimmy Carter was not President-elect until November 1976, Elvis's Carter connection went as far back as at least 1973, when Carter was governor of Georgia. A well-publicized photograph shows Elvis with the governor and Mrs. Carter. Governor Carter subsequently proclaimed January 8, 1974, Elvis Presley Day in Georgia. Taking all of the above into consideration, it is clear that both President Nixon and President Carter held Elvis Presley in high esteem. Government files prove that Elvis spoke with President Carter at the White House two weeks before August 16, 1977. This telephone call was not only private but was arranged by an agent of the FBI.

Two weeks after this private conversation—upon hearing that Elvis had "died"—President Carter issued this tribute: "Elvis

Presley's death deprives our country of a part of itself. He was unique; and irreplaceable. More than twenty years ago he burst upon the scene with an impact that was unprecedented and will probably never be equaled. His music and his personality, fusing the styles of white country and black rhythm and blues, permanently changed the face of American popular culture. His following was immense and he was a symbol to people the world over, of the vitality, rebelliousness, and good humor of his country."

Journalists, in noting this tribute, commented that for the President of the United States to issue a formal statement was unusual. Of course, no one at that time knew about Operation Fountain Pen, nor about Elvis's calls to the White House, nor of President Carter's calls to Elvis.

(In a later chapter, Elvis's role regarding Operation Fountain Pen is more fully discussed, proving that Elvis's position with the DEA, as well as his status with the FBI and CIA, were of major importance.)

"It is obvious to us that no one in Elvis's group of 'friends' knew of this special undercover agent and the role Elvis played in setting up his cover," Maria Columbus's newsletter further states with regard to the Pritchett letter(s). "Since Elvis had an undercover agent in this group from 1974 to 1976 when did he find the time to do drugs himself?" Maria makes a valid point, especially if one considers that many of Elvis's friends often wondered if Elvis faked "being whacked out." Could it be that in order to gain the confidence of drug dealers Elvis may have faked being a drug user? Have other undercover agents used this same technique?

Don't dismiss the possibility until you read this entire book.

We also know from government files that Elvis visited FBI headquarters on December 31, 1970. Although Elvis did not meet with J. Edgar Hoover, he and his group, which included William N. Morris, former Sheriff of Shelby County, Tennessee, and six others, were given a tour of FBI facilities. Less than a week after Elvis's visit with the FBI, Elvis received a personal letter from J. Edgar Hoover, thanking Elvis for the offer of the confidential assistance Elvis had extended to the bureau. We know that Elvis never had any FBI credentials, but whether the FBI ever took Elvis up on his offer of help is not now a matter of public record—if it is on record at all, it may exist in unreleased FBI files. Obviously if Elvis, or any agent for that matter, did work in a confidential manner with various arms of the government, such information would not be expected to be readily available.

Two months prior to Elvis's December 1970 meeting with President Nixon, Elvis was presented with a CNOA membership certificate that states: "This is to certify that Elvis A. Presley is a member in good standing of the California Narcotics Officers Association." Once again we have to ask: What was Elvis doing previous to his meeting with President Nixon to earn him this award—beyond Elvis's other nomination, as one of the Ten Outstanding Young Men of the year?

It's also true that Elvis had badges from other law-enforcement agencies. Some were honorary, others were not. In his wallet Elvis carried a badge from the Memphis police force. Several biographies tell of the time Elvis went after a man accused of stealing from him. He used his federal narcotics badge to stop a commercial airplane at the Las Vegas airport by racing out on the tarmac as the plane taxied, flashing his badge up to the pilot in the cockpit. The pilot immediately lowered the gangplank and allowed Elvis to board. After checking out the passengers and discovering the man he was after was not on board, Elvis thanked the pilot and "waved him on."

Elvis was also a member of the National Sheriffs' Association, headquartered in Washington, D.C. Shelby County Sheriff William "Bill" Morris presented Elvis with his identification card as a law officer. In published interviews Morris has stated that Elvis was very vocal about situations that were anti-law enforcement. Elvis also played a major role in the establishment of drug-abuse centers in Denver and Los Angeles. Morris says a program had been discussed whereby all law-enforcement agencies throughout the United States would develop a program for older scouts called "The Elvis Presley Law Enforcement Specialty Post," funded by the Elvis Presley Foundation. One of this post's purposes would be to help young people establish positive attitudes toward law enforcement. Elvis felt if he could help the youth respect the law, his job fighting the war on drugs would be easier.

Sheriff Morris, who accompanied Elvis to FBI headquarters in late 1970, was also instrumental in Elvis's being named by the Jaycees one of the Ten Most Outstanding Young Men in America in January 1971. In general, Elvis did not go in for awards. However, Sheriff Morris said in an interview that Elvis believed the Junior Chamber of Commerce was one of the most involved groups of men in the free world. Usually this particular honor goes to a scholar, scientist, or politician. Elvis was the first entertainer to receive such a high award, an award he accepted with pride, saying it was one of the great achievements of his life.

As was earlier mentioned, it was George Bush who praised Elvis during the Jaycee ceremony. The following article appeared in a Memphis newspaper in January 1971: "A hectic day of Jaycee activities yesterday was highlighted by a luncheon speech from United Nations Ambassador-Appointee George Bush and last by the organization's awards ceremony honoring the Ten Outstanding Young Men in America. He praised his audience as 'men who have thought new thoughts and rejected old dogmas. But to guarantee this country never accepts the violent answer our people must be willing to work within the system.' He complimented the Jaycees on their Top Ten selection and told Memphis to 'watch out if Elvis Presley ever decided to enter politics. They would have to regroup their forces,' he said."

Thus Elvis Presley had connections not only with two U.S. Presidents, but with three: President Richard M. Nixon, President Jimmy Carter, and President George Bush.

Elvis also said something worth examining in his acceptance speech to the Jaycees: "I've always been a dreamer. I read comic books and I was the hero of the comic book. I saw movies and I was the hero in the movie. So every dream that I ever dreamed has come true a hundred times. These gentlemen over here, you see, these type of people who care, are dedicated, you realize, is it not possible that they might be building the Kingdom of Heaven? It's not too far-fetched from reality. I'd like to say that I learned very early in life that without a song the day would never end, without a song a man ain't got a friend, without a song the road would never bend, without a song. So I'll keep singing a song."

If indeed "the child is the father of the man," this childhood belief of Presley's in a comic-book hero could well have played a psychological role in the man-Elvis who would, almost single-handedly, want to come to the aid of his country if called upon.

As further proof that Elvis's appointment as a federal agent with the DEA was legitimate, Elvis's friend and spiritual advisor, Larry Geller, pointed out in his book *If I Can Dream: Elvis' Own Story* (New York: Simon & Schuster, 1989) that he was with Elvis in June of 1977 during Elvis's last concert tour. The two men were in Elvis's hotel room at the Netherland Hilton in Cincinnati; Elvis showed Larry a small black book issued each year by the U.S. Justice Department in which the only names listed are those of narcotics agents. He told Larry that only agents are given a copy of the black book and, as only agents are listed—Elvis was proud to show Larry his listing in the book. As he had often done before, Elvis spoke about his love of America as well as his willingness to help his country in any way possible.

Once Elvis became an agent with the DEA, he began to surround himself with law-enforcement officials, such as John O'Grady, who had been in charge of the narcotics division of the Los Angeles Police Department. At around the same time Elvis became committed to law enforcement he hired Dick Grob, a former sergeant with the Palm Springs police. Thus during the 1970s it is clear that Elvis was a federal agent, that he was giving cover in his band to another agent, and was surrounded by two lawmen in top security positions.

The logical question now is: Was Elvis afraid of something or someone?

Returning to Larry Geller's book *If I Can Dream*, the author reports that Presley fell asleep only to awake mumbling his daughter's name, warning her to stay away from a trap. When Larry asked Elvis what was frightening him, Elvis was evasive, ending with the statement that he wanted Lisa at Graceland as soon as the June 1977 tour was completed.

Geller was also witness to a telephone call Elvis received some months earlier, on December 31, 1976, from President-elect Jimmy Carter. The call lasted about ten minutes. Elvis told Larry that Carter had asked for a meeting with him at the White House after the inauguration. Carter wanted to appoint Elvis as special advisor to him on the youth of America, the music scene, and "other projects."

Elvis told Larry: "President Carter is planning to create a special post for me. I promised him I would serve my country and use whatever influence I had, especially with the war on drugs."

Why didn't this happen? What was occurring between late 1976 and 1977 that prevented Elvis from accepting this post? I believe the answer to these questions lies within the FBI's undercover operative, Operation Fountain Pen. While perusing the FBI files on Pen, it became painfully clear that Elvis Presley was involved in something so dangerous that even a comic-book hero could not escape. Elvis was not only fearful for his own life, but also feared that his friends and family, especially his little daughter, could come into grave danger.

With this in mind, I believe history will prove that Elvis Aron Presley, beyond being an incomparable American entertainer, is in reality an American hero.

* * *

To peruse FBI files on Elvis Presley, write:

Freedom of Information—Privacy Acts Section
Records Management Division/U.S. Department of Justice
Federal Bureau of Investigation
Washington, D.C. 10535
Subject requested: Elvis Aron Presley
Freedom of Information Act (Title 5, U.S. Code, Section 552)

The DEA badge President Nixon presented to Elvis was displayed in the Trophy Room museum at Graceland on the wall behind glass among many law enforcement badges Elvis owned. As of late 1996, the badge has a new special shelf display in the living room.

3

THE THINKER

Many Elvis skeptics have commented they don't believe Elvis had the type of intelligence required—or was even intelligent enough—to have led the double life of an entertainer and a federal agent. Yet everyone I've spoken to who knew Elvis says how truly intelligent a man Elvis was, that his thinking ran very deep, especially regarding his private religious studies. According to singer T.G. Sheppard, Elvis was not only an avid reader but also had an amazing memory.

During a guest spot on KGO Talk Radio in San Francisco, TV/radio personality and comedian Marty Allen also spoke of Elvis's intelligence. "Elvis was one of the nicest men I knew. He was the kind of man who could find humor in anything. I asked him once how he could do that in sad situations and he told me that if he didn't, then he would not be able to cope. Elvis also had this ability to read lips," Marty added. "He would be listening to you and talking and also reading the conversation across the room! He often shocked people by knowing what was going on all around him. He used to play down his intelligence, preferring that people did not know how smart he really was."

Besides his lip-reading talents, Elvis was a master of disguises. And since the act of disguising in itself means to change appearance and identity—evidence of the secrecy that Elvis apparently enjoyed—then it is highly possible Elvis disguised himself more often than anyone was aware. After all, if Elvis could sneak away from family and friends and go to Washington, D.C. to see the President of the United States, certainly lesser outings were possible. Perhaps those times he was "reclused in his room" with a "Do Not Disturb" sign were not what they appeared.

Would this type of game playing fall in line with the psyche of a man who dreamed of comic-book heroes? Actually, when Elvis disguised himself as Elvis, most people didn't believe it. Close friend and aide Charlie Hodge was quoted in a fan periodical as he described a time Elvis tried unsuccessfully to convince a throng of people outside a Memphis club that he was really Elvis Presley. No one believed that the real Elvis would be out in public. Another pre-1977 story revolves around a Memphis theater that held an audition for Elvis-lookalikes-soundalikes. Elvis got such a kick out of the "Elvis-Call" that he decided to put on his best Elvis outfit—capes and rings—and go to the theater. Once there he mingled freely with his "clones," doing his best "Hey, baby…" Afterward, Elvis came back to the mansion at Graceland in hysterics. Everyone thought it was equally funny that the real Elvis went unrecognized. "Yeah, but you haven't heard the best part," Elvis said, laughing. "I tried out— and lost!"

Several have written about the time Elvis was convinced to go out on a Las Vegas street midday with the bet that no one would make a big deal of it. Elvis did go out there in broad daylight. He stood for some time leaning against a building. People walked by. Some looked, others did not. Those who did a double-take paused but then continued on, no doubt thinking, "Nah. Can't be…"

Elvis did disguise himself in Denver during a trip to Vail, Colorado, to look for a house. He wore a ski mask and a jumpsuit while making an offer. The bid was rejected by the owner, who was unaware of Elvis's identity. At other times Elvis wore police uniforms in public—once in a restaurant. On this occasion Elvis was recognized, but when people asked him if he was Elvis, he replied, "Nah. Everyone gets me confused with him." At other times Elvis was said to don a blond wig. Another incident involves Elvis's manager Colonel Tom Parker hunting all over for a "disappearing" Elvis while they were at the airport waiting to board a plane to

Denver. Finally found, Elvis was down on his hands and knees pitching pennies with a taxi driver.

In their book *Elvis: What Happened?* (New York: Ballantine Books, 1977), Dave Hebler, Red West, and Sonny West talk about a time when Elvis went out on a drug bust with a Memphis narcotics officer. In order to disguise himself, Elvis put on a jumpsuit. Over the jumpsuit he put on a snowsuit. Over his face he put on a ski mask. On top of that he put on a hat. Hebler and the Wests say Elvis stood out like a neon sign.

Although Elvis's face was and is one of the most recognizable in the world, he could indeed go "underground." For one, Elvis probably has more lookalikes than any other man on this planet; as proven, Elvis was actually able to walk around looking like Elvis and get away with it, especially if he wore sunglasses, his sideburns and hair kept dark and long, and dressed in a typical Elvis costume.

Obviously Elvis enjoyed game playing, even to the point of being able to fake his death successfully—this prior to August 16, 1977—as illustrated by an incident in *Elvis: What Happened?* Faking unconsciousness, even pretending to be dead, was a trick Elvis had used several times. According to Red West there was a time when Elvis was performing and he began to look sick. Staggering offstage, he collapsed. He was taken to the hospital, where the doctors told everyone to leave Elvis and return to the motel to await word. Red says they went back to the motel waiting for the worst. Around one in the morning there was a knock at Red's door. "Damn, man, if it ain't that old sonofabitch Elvis standing there healthier than a herd of cattle, and he is grinning from ear to ear. Not a doggone thing wrong with him. We all pump him full of questions, and he tells us he is now okay. But when the other boys return to their rooms, Elvis makes a confession to me. The whole collapsing routine was just a big act..."

Red recounts another instance: "I remember," says Red, "one time we were in a hotel in Colorado, and he [Elvis] called my room and told me to come see him, that there was something he wanted to talk to me about. Well, I got straight to his room and Elvis is laying out of it on the floor. I thought, oh well, he just whacked himself out with something. So I undressed him and put him in bed and covered him up. But later I got to thinking. When he spoke to me on the telephone, he was completely straight, like he hadn't taken a thing, and I got to that room in less than a couple of minutes. Now no drug hits you that hard. So then I suspected he wasn't asleep or out of it at all. He was wide awake and just faking it, just to see how I would handle him. He tested us a lot of times like that."

Stories such as these, told by many of Elvis's Memphis mafia, make even the most naïve wonder if Elvis was ever truly "whacked out," as has been sometimes reported. Such occasions could easily be examples of Elvis putting to practice another theory of his involving mind-over-body techniques, or perhaps these methods were means of eavesdropping on those close to him, checking their loyalty, listening to what was being said. What is apparent is that Elvis was able to use his body as a decoy—at will he could make his physical condition appear to be other than what might be supposed by an outside observer.

If so, the question is: How often did Elvis practice this sort of routine? Could he have heard conversations while in this condition—conversations that may have led to the firing of close friends, rather than the reported payroll-reduction rationale? Or could it be that Elvis wanted those close to him to believe that he was whacked out on one drug or another for reasons only Elvis knew?

A few years prior to Elvis's "death" there was another faked-death episode on the part of prankster Elvis. This involved not only Red and Sonny West but also J.D. Sumner and the Stamps Quartet. The plot was to tell J.D. Sumner and his group that a madman was after Elvis with a gun. To put the plan into motion three security guards were recruited to act out a fake gunfight with an assassin. Sonny was to be the assassin and carry a gun loaded with blanks. He would remain hidden. Everyone, including the security guards, emptied their guns and loaded them with blanks, and informed J.D. Sumner that a madman was loose.

In the suite J.D. began checking inside doors. He and the Stamps were understandably nervous about what might happen. Sonny soon left on one or another premise, leaving J.D. Sumner and the Stamps by the bar talking to Elvis and the security guards. Soon Sonny, who had sneaked back in, reached around a corner and started shouting and firing away, with Red shooting back. The next fusillade of shots appeared to cut down the security guards. It looked like a mass slaughter, with those "in on it" falling dead. Those not in on it were hysterical, running, shouting, screaming, hiding. J.D. even threw himself over Elvis's prone body. Even when it became clear, after Elvis began to laugh convulsively, that the whole faked death scene was just that, J.D. and his group remained terror-stricken.

Red made a point of saying they could have won Oscars.

Was this a rehearsal for one of the greatest theatrical roles of Elvis's life?

As for the drug stories themselves: Most who knew Elvis agree that he did not take street drugs but that he did overindulge in prescription drugs. However, Elvis knew his drugs, knew which one mixed with another. He was known to have taken prescribed sedatives for sleep. There were times Elvis performed while sick, one time with the flu, at other times with a temperature. Most of his tours were grueling to the point of exhaustion.

"Last week I was sick for a day," Elvis said during one performance. "I had 102 temperature. I had the flu and missed two shows. They said I hadn't been sick but that I was strung out on drugs. I heard from three different sources that I'm dependent on heroin. Never in my life have I been strung out. They don't give a black belt if you're on drugs. Reports like this hurt my daughter, my family, everyone..."

Displaying a certificate to the audience, Elvis continued: "This is from the International Narcotics Enforcement Association. This certificate gives me special honors and a lifelong membership. I've been wearing a federal narcotics badge for six years. They don't give you that if you're strung out."

Still, no matter how Elvis protested, the rumors had begun: Elvis took drugs. Yet when one examines the big picture, especially since this speech to his audience was given in 1976 (during the time of the

Operation Fountain Pen FBI operative), when Elvis's involvement might have cost him his life, those same rumors may have been his cloak of protection. After all, who would suspect a drugged entertainer of being a federal agent?

It would be well to make a point here that shortly before 1977 Elvis told J.D. Sumner and other members of his entourage that he wouldn't be performing as much the following year as he had been and that they should look for other work. Some questioned Elvis as to what he actually meant. He just stood by his statement: "Look for other work."

It was evident that Elvis had begun "to clean house." What was not evident was why. This was about the time he fired Red and Sonny West, and Dave Hebler. All of them had been with Elvis for years, with Red going all the way back to high school. Little by little, one by one, the Memphis mafia would be no more.

Red, Sonny, and Dave never understood why they had been let go. And, since it was well recognized that Elvis was a born planner, what Elvis was doing just didn't make sense. It was obvious, then: Elvis was fashioning major changes in his life, and his ultimate plans were being kept secret. (Many biographers note that Elvis Presley possessed an uncanny sense of timing—almost perfection. Elvis chalked this up to having studied numerology: Certain plans would be successful if enacted at a particular time. If not, they could easily fall apart.)

Yet as secretive as Elvis was, his conversations from early to middle 1977 were laced with what could be perceived as "hints." At one point Elvis told Larry Geller that he wanted to become a monk, and that the life he was leading had to end, that it had "gone on far too long." Elvis spoke about seeking a higher purpose, of doing more with his life, and that his destiny had not been met.

Besides making suggestive comments to Larry Geller, Elvis left other signs that changes were going to be made:

· In many of his spiritual books, Elvis underlined or even wrote in his own hand the following words: "Should I return, you would not recognize me."

- Elvis began saying "adios" at the end of his shows.
- During his last concert tour just weeks before his "death," Elvis turned toward his stepbrother and said: "Know what, Rick? I may not look good for my television special tonight, but I'll look good in my coffin."
- On his final concert tour, Elvis, with his eyes away from his audience, looked down and said: "I am and I was."

Beyond saying strange things and even saying good-bye to friends and family, it appeared that Elvis-the-songmaster may have left tantalizing messages in his songs:

- Elvis insisted that one of the titles recorded during his last studio sessions be: "The Last Farewell."
- Elvis launched his version of the song "My Way" toward the end, yet despite knowing the lyrics well, he deliberately stopped and read each word during a final concert—almost as if to stress the lyrics rather than the singing. (Rick Stanley reported that although Elvis liked the song "My Way," he never made it a part of his show until the last year.)
- The lyrics in the *Moody Blue* album may contain a clue to Elvis's plans: "I'll be coming home, wait for me."
- When Wayne Newton talked about his last conversation with Elvis, in which Elvis said, "Go on. Just remember, it's all yours now, all yours…," was that also a clue? (Newton later said in an interview that Elvis seemed to "know he was going to die and that his choice of songs at the end was his way of saying good-bye to the world—every song was his Swan Song.")
- "And now the end is near," Elvis both read and sang before the grand finale, "I'll do it my way…" (during a rendition of the song "My Way").

Perhaps in the end that is exactly what Elvis did.

4
DOUBLE-A

There were other clues that may indicate Elvis was trying to tell the world he was leaving. Perhaps most provocative was the body itself in the coffin, a picture of which appeared on the front page of *The National Enquirer*. What surprised a good many people was how young and slim Elvis looked and how "pugged" Elvis's nose appeared. Since Elvis had a beautiful, classic nose, response from family and friends about this oddity was that Elvis fell on his face because he had a heart attack. Most people do fall forward in such circumstances, but the body's weight does not rest on the nose as if it were the point of a spinning top. If that were the case, people who sleep on their faces should have pugged noses.

The following quotation from Maria Columbus's fan-club newsletter *The Elvis Special* came from LaCosta, sister of singer Tanya Tucker: "We were right up to his casket and stood there, and God, I couldn't believe it. He looked just like a piece of plastic laying there. He didn't look like him at all…he looked more like a dummy than a real person. You know a lot of people think it was a dummy. They don't think he's dead."

Larry Geller also commented that Elvis looked like a piece of clay.

Others, like Gene Smith, spoke about the "beads of sweat" on the body in the coffin. Since dead bodies do not sweat, this raises legitimate questions. (When I was a guest on Larry King's TV show, I spoke with Elvis's right-hand man, Joe Esposito, who also acknowledged the beads of sweat. He blew this off by saying it was very hot that day.

Hot or not, dead bodies do not sweat. But wax will bead up in the heat.

One can argue that, if Elvis wanted to escape from his lifestyle, why the open coffin? Why the circuslike viewing and funeral? My answer, especially after reading the FBI files and documents pertaining to the Pen operative, is that it was essential for the world at large to see that Elvis Presley was indeed dead—even if the body in the casket did appear to be a younger, slimmer Elvis.

After all, Elvis said, only weeks before, "I know I look fat now and I'll look terrible for my TV special coming up. But I'll tell you this: I'll look good in my casket."

Every one of us has a bit of vanity. If you have to go to all the trouble of having a waxen image made of you, why not have one that looks younger and slimmer?

Although the official announcement did not come until 3:30 PM on August 16, 1977, Elvis was said to have died at around 2:00 PM, at least an hour and a half earlier. Since the body was to be on display the next day, August 17, and the funeral was scheduled for August 18, Vernon Presley had quite a lot to do—especially trying for a sick man, which indeed he was. Yet the speed with which all arrangements were made is mind-boggling in itself, particularly when one considers the following duties that were accomplished in this time frame: an autopsy and embalming were completed; the body was back at the Memphis Funeral Home around 8:00 PM; sixteen white limousines were ordered; a white Cadillac hearse was readied; a specially designed casket was ordered and flown in; a casket blanket of five hundred red roses was made; security and police were ordered; the planned concert tour was canceled; personal calls were made by Vernon to fan club presidents asking that they not attend; clothing was chosen; songs and singers were chosen, ministers contacted, the procession charted—and the body put on private display by 11:30 the next morning.

The planned public viewing by the press and crying fans would take place a few hours later. The casket was moved from the living room to the foyer of the front entrance of Graceland. At 3:00 PM, according to the Memphis *Commercial Appeal*, "the floodgates at the end of the long driveway were opened to the thousands who flowed like a river past the lifeless body…"

At 6:30 PM the gates were closed.

Another letter from one of my readers came with the following information: "I personally know the man who made Elvis's coffin. He said it was really bizarre. It was a rush order, it was copper, but it had three lids! The first that would go over was double, then there was another single one piece that went over that, and finally a single copper to go over everything! He also said that there was no way Elvis's body weight and the weight of the coffin was 900 pounds. Something else was in it. He did say it was big enough to put an air-conditioner in it…" (Recall Gene Smith said the coffin was so heavy he fell to his knees.)

However, the most significant after-death clue revolves around the fact that Elvis's middle name is misspelled on the gravestone at Graceland. Rather than Aron (single-A spelling) the gravestone reads: Elvis Aaron Presley (double-A spelling).

Yet directly outside the gates of Graceland was the marker erected by the Elvis Presley International Memorial Foundation and authorized by the Shelby County Historical Society, which read: Elvis Aron Presley. Since this marker was presented five years after the "death" of Elvis—August 16, 1982—this belies the rumor that Elvis may have legally changed his middle name while he lived. However, suddenly and without apparent explanation, a new marker was erected around 1996 that now reads "Aaron."

Who ordered the new spelling? And why? Could it be that Elvis now chooses to live as Elvis Aaron so as to increase his spiritual vibrations according to numerology? (See Chapter 5.) Keep in mind that he also added another letter to his twin Jesse Garon's name, now reading Jessie Garon.

Patsy Guy Hammontree, assistant professor of English at the University of Tennessee, in her extensively researched work *Elvis Presley: A Bio-Bibliography* (Westport, CT: Greenwood Press, 1985) affirms Elvis's middle name as being spelled "Aron," with his twin brother's name spelled "Jesse Garon." (Jesse Garon's marker at Graceland is also misspelled, reading "Jessie Garon Presley." As with Elvis's name having had an extra letter added, someone decided that

Elvis's twin's name would also have an extra letter.) *The Elvis Catalog* (New York: Dolphin/Double-day, 1987) by Lee Cotten, a noted Elvis scholar, uses the single-A spelling.

Further evidence that Elvis never changed the spelling of his middle name is demonstrated via the note of appreciation that Elvis's family sent out after Elvis's death: "The family of Elvis Aron Presley acknowledges with grateful appreciation your kind expression of sympathy."

Additionally, why would Elvis want to change the spelling of his middle name in the first place, especially when it was his beloved mother who chose the single-A spelling? Gladys wanted Aron spelled this way because of Jesse Garon; she wanted Elvis to know always, by looking at "Aron," that he was a part of "Garon."

When I had lunch years ago with Vester Presley, Vernon's brother and Elvis's uncle, he verified that Elvis always used the single A. He didn't seem particularly upset by the misspelling on the grave, and in fact said his nephew's name was misspelled on other graves at Graceland as well. With a twinkle in his eye, he jokingly said, "I guess the gravemaker made the mistake. Probably too expensive to change…"

Although the majority of fans and fan publications already agree that the "Aron" spelling is the correct spelling, let's take it step by step (all documents and other materials listed below follow the single-A spelling):

SINGLE-A

- Elvis's birth certificate, the one on display at Graceland and sold as a souvenir, reads: Elvis Aron Presley.
- All other legal documents use "Aron."
- Memphis city schools and Humes High School diploma.
- Social security card (on display at Graceland).
- Army induction and discharge papers.
- Elvis's army duffel bag (on display at Graceland).
- RCA contracts.
- Records and music albums.

- Promotional materials.
- Awards.
- Law-enforcement applications.
- Marriage certificate.
- Elvis's Bible.
- Aron Music.
- Medical examiner's report.
- Crossword puzzles.
- Elvis catalogues and bibliographies.
- Memorial plaques.
- And last but not least, Elvis's own signature. Who should know more about how his name is spelled than the man himself?

Without running down an encyclopedia's worth of facts and other tidbits to prove that Elvis's middle name is spelled "Aron," and not "Aaron," I've instead presented visuals to support my point. There's literally nothing, other than mistakes made by journalists, to indicate that Elvis ever used the double-A spelling. So why the mistakes on the graves?

My initial turn of thought (as first proposed in my *Is Elvis Alive?* book) is the rationale that, if one were not dead, one could beat out superstition by purposely misspelling one's name on the grave—as a way of not putting a hex on oneself. I later learned that it was Elvis himself who asked his father to misspell the middle name, which is intriguing. Why would Elvis instruct his father, ill and years older than Elvis, as to what should be put on Elvis's own tombstone unless Elvis knew he would "die" fairly soon? Just some sort of psychic whim? And if Elvis truly wanted to depart as "Aaron," why didn't Elvis use that spelling while "alive"? Or is it possible that "the singer-Aron" departed on August 16, 1977, while the "messenger-of-God-Aaron" was given new life?

Too farfetched? Not when you study Elvis's intense interest in the science of numbers and spirituality. (**AUTHOR'S NOTE:** Please see Chapters 5 through 7 of this book for a discussion of Elvis's pursuits in numerology and spirituality.)

In Elvis's way of thinking, his "death" could also mean "being born anew." If Elvis did indeed add another letter to his name, it would change the power of his numbers, particularly if Aron became Aaron—which would change Elvis's soul number (3), giving to him a "personal self."

Since Elvis was an identical twin, his brother's name would have to be changed as well. Elvis always said he felt a part of "himself" missing, that his brother had died so that he could live. "I feel because identical twins come from one egg they share a twin soul," he was heard to say. "If one twin dies at birth, his soul goes back into the living twin—therefore twice the power, twice the fame; twice the sorrow, twice the pain…"

If Elvis added another letter to his name to change his soul number, would he not have had to add another letter to his dead twin's name in order to keep them spiritually aligned? How could the same soul have its energy pattern split? Although this may seem irrelevant to those who know little about Elvis's spirituality, those who do know the intensity of his studies realize that this would be in line with Elvis's thinking. Remember, all historical documentation states that Elvis's twin was named Jesse Garon. It's spelled that way every place except on the stone(s) at Graceland.

The memorial plaque at Graceland reads: In Memory of Jessie Garon Presley.

Gladys's Graceland stone reads: Gladys Love Smith Presley, Mother of Elvis Aaron Presley and Jessie Garon Presley.

Gladys's Graceland stone might well be expected to read: Gladys Love Smith Presley, Mother of Elvis Aron Presley and Jesse Garon Presley. These were the sons Gladys gave birth to and to whom she gave rhyming middle names.

Why the changes?

With an extra letter added to each name, had Elvis given both his brother (who lived within him and through him) and himself a chance for a "second" life?

There is something else puzzling about the graves at Graceland—besides these misspellings. I doubt anyone would argue that Elvis adored his mother. Everyone who knew him said he was devastated by her death, that he wanted to be with her, that he always said he would be buried beside her. However, upon visiting Graceland, you can see that Elvis's stone is between his father and grandmother rather than beside Gladys. There is no valid reason for going against Elvis's known wishes to be buried beside his mother—unless no one is actually buried at Graceland, including Elvis.

I've received thousands of letters regarding both the spelling on the graves and their placement; a portion of one of these pieces of correspondence follows:

"I am the mother of two sons—my youngest, Dan, became a very good friend of one of the Presley cousins. Now, the Presley cousins trust few people, usually because someone always wanted something. They were used. But my son became close to all the remaining Presleys, particularly Jimmy Gamble. He is Vester Presley's grandson. Patsy Gamble worked as Elvis's secretary and did many other things. She was always at the mansion; so was Vester, as he once was a guard at the gate. My son played touch football on the grounds of Graceland, swam in the pool…Gail, you talk about Elvis's middle name being misspelled on the gravestone. You ask why? I know why. He [Jimmy] told my son that Elvis was not buried there. My son looked at him and said, 'Well, if not there, where?' He said, 'Oh, well, only the family knows.'"

Obviously one could argue that even if no one was buried at Graceland, that in itself does nothing to prove that Elvis is alive. The absence of any physical bodies at the Graceland grounds could simply be the result of a security concern.

But that still doesn't explain why the names are misspelled.

When Gladys died, with deliberation and thought, Elvis had the Star of David and the Christian cross added to his mother's memorial plaque at Forest Hill Cemetery. One reason was that Elvis's spiritual studies embraced a universal God. Elvis also wore the Star of David and a cross. Neither of these symbols is on the stones at Graceland.

"My husband and I have been to Graceland and visited Elvis's grave," wrote a fan from Illinois. "We do not believe Elvis or family members are buried there, because I have been taught you bury a human body facing east and west according to the Bible. Elvis and his family members' headstones are facing north and south."

(According to the Bible, one's head should rest in the west, one's feet in the east, the body in effect facing east; thus, when Resurrection Day comes, the departed will face the Face of God. I called several mortuaries and they said it is traditional to bury a body facing east, especially in the South. "I don't know of any church cemetery not burying facing east; even memorial parks try to hold to this tradition," was their general response.)

Elvis and his family read the Bible religiously, studied it. They were fundamentalists. Why are the graves the opposite of Biblical declaratives? (Gladys's original grave in Forest Hill did face east.)

Another clue?

Finally, I received another interesting letter from a woman who said she and her friend attended the Tenth Anniversary Tribute Week in Memphis, arriving a few days prior to August 16, 1987, for sightseeing. Forest Hill Cemetery was on their tour. It was early morning and they wandered about. A man walked toward them wearing a baseball cap and sunglasses, with gray hair, no sideburns, normal clothing, head down. They nodded, but then, as the man passed, they suddenly stopped and stared at each other in shock. "It was Elvis Presley, I swear it," the woman wrote. "But we talked ourselves out of it, thinking: No, it's impossible. So we continued on, only to learn that we were heading in the direction of where Elvis's mother had been buried. It was the morning of August 14, 1987. August 14th is the day Elvis Presley's mother died. Could it be possible…?"

Could it…?

5

NUMBERS

In order to understand how it is possible for Elvis to do what he may have done—faked his own death—it is essential to understand the role numerology and astrology played in his life. Numerology is the science of numbers as related to the secret patterns involving the universe—nature's own calculations—which frequently relate to the spiritual side of things. In writings about numerology, many of the universe's secret patterns are expressed through the position and movement of stars and other heavenly bodies—thus the strong link between astrology and numerology.

Numerology was used originally by the Egyptians, who were considered masters of the hidden meaning of numbers; their application of the science of numbers was toward time and its relationship to human life. Elvis was always attracted to Egyptian history and artifacts; in fact there are many crystal pyramids on tables at Graceland. Those who study pyramid power claim this three-dimensional shape is the most perfect power possible, having a direct relationship to the power of the sun and to the entire cosmos. The original city of Memphis was an ancient capital of Egypt. With its heartland along the grand river Nile, Egypt remains home to many of the world's most revered pyramid constructions.

A giant gleaming pyramid was later built along the Mississippi river waterfront in Memphis, Tennessee—America's namesake city of the pharaonic metropolis, situated beside America's own mother of waters. The pyramid at Memphis, Tennessee, opened to the public in 1991. One of the investors in the Memphis pyramid is head of Graceland. Exhibits keyed to the life and career of Elvis Presley are among the main attractions at the Memphis pyramid.

Not only did Elvis wear pyramid-like symbols on his costumes, but he wore the sun symbol as well. Because Elvis was an intense student of spirituality and numerology, his appreciation of symbols and the powers they held was equally intense.

The sun played a prominent role in Egyptology—as it played a prominent role in Elvis's life: Elvis recorded his first record at Memphis-based Sun Studios in August, the month of the sun.

Elvis's resplendent "sundial" suit is another example of the prominent role this celestial symbol played in Elvis's life. The sundial suit displays a design based on the famous Aztec sun-calendar stone (the original stone is on exhibit in Mexico City's Museum of Anthropology). As with Egypt, the Aztec civilization was a kingdom of the sun and, like many cultures of ancient Mexico, the Aztecs had an age-old tradition of pyramid building, and were adept in the study of numbers and the stars.

In 1977, during his last two tours, this sundial suit was the only ensemble Elvis wore onstage. He would wear nothing else. His sundial suit features a sundial with sixteen points on the back and, divided down the front, eight points on either side of his chest. It is said Elvis wore this suit exactly forty-two times. (Forty-two is the age at which Elvis "died.")

Elvis entered his career in August, the month of the sun, and left it in the same month of the sun. Numerologically speaking, Elvis made his exit as a number eight, and almost instantaneously became a number seven, a number with a decrease in vibration.

This transformation occurred when "Aron" became "Aaron." In numerology, letters of the alphabet are each given number values; the numerological significance of any particular name is based on the number values of the letters that form that name (be it a full name, family name, or nickname).

To get a sense of the sorts of messages connected with certain numbers—let's take a look at the number seven. (This is the number Elvis would have become with the double-A spelling of his middle name.) Throughout the Bible, as well as in other sacred books, the number seven always relates to the God-force:

SIGNIFICANCE OF THE NUMBER 7

- The seven days (or cycles) of the Genesis creation.
- The seven heavens.
- The seven thrones.
- The seven seals.
- The seven churches.
- The seventh day.

The Bible speaks of the seven generations from David to the birth of Christ. The biblical Book of Revelation speaks of the seven spirits of God sent forth into all the earth. The prophet Ezekiel speaks of the seven angels of the Lord that go to and fro throughout the whole earth—a reference to the influences of the seven creative planets that radiate through the earth. Egyptian religion refers to seven spirits, as do other religious traditions ranging from Hindu to Greek to Hebrew.

All state that the number seven is the God-force. Seven is the only number capable of dividing the number of eternity. The seven days of the week have been the outcome of the influence of the seven creative planets. I would suggest that for those who want to further understand the mystery and power of numbers that they read *Cheiro's Book of Numbers* (New York: Arco Publishing, 1964). This book as well as the Bible were carried by Elvis wherever he traveled and were the two books that were always on his nightstand.

Ironically, these two books were found to be missing from his nightstand only hours after his "death."

In numerology, each letter of the alphabet has an assigned number; these letter numbers may be calculated and interpreted on several different levels. In *Cheiro's*, Elvis's name number equals nine, but his vibration number is eight, one of the most powerful vibrations in the theory of numerology. (Eight turned sideways is the symbol for infinity.)

Elvis's compound number could change, depending upon whether he used "Aron" or "Aaron" as the spelling of his middle name. By adding the second A, Elvis could have changed the power of his name numbers as well as his vibration number. Because this is a rather complicated and personal matter, it is best dealt with here only lightly in order to point out that it was of intense interest to Elvis and may well explain why the names on the graves have an added letter.

From a numerology reading:

> Basically, Elvis was born a number eight—and was born in a number eight period of the Zodiac. He needed to decrease his vibrations in order to have a happier life. Number eight people "suffer the greatest losses," greater than any other numbers. Number eight people are generally misunderstood; they are very lonely people at heart, and because of this develop fears of mistrust and increase their potential of being used. Love is rarely given to a number eight individual in pure form. It is usually given for greed, lust, or advancement of self-gain. This is the biggest reason Elvis chose a life in exile. He wanted to study, meditate, educate his soul, learn, travel, and regain losses financially. Elvis's love is music. I predict he will return to the people and the public eye. He sings and feels from the soul, and the people will see him in a different light when he returns. He is a teacher in his own right and has a lot of work left to do.

The month of August—the eighth month of the calendar year—was undoubtedly the most favorable month for Elvis to put into action the most important plans of his life: the leaving of one life to begin "another." August was also the month that his beloved mother, Gladys, to whom Elvis was psychically and spiritually connected, left this world for "another." It's reasonable to assume that if Elvis were looking at the month of August as a leaving point, he would have chosen August 14, 1977, the day of his mother's death. However, August 14 did not contain the vibrational power that August 16 held. Elvis did begin to fast on August 14, perhaps using his mother's death as the date to begin the process of "cleaning house."

Other numbers held special meaning for Elvis in different ways: For instance, Elvis used the theme music from the film *2001: A Space Odyssey* (directed by Stanley Kubrick, from a book by Arthur C. Clarke) as introductory fanfare to his stage show late in his career. That theme music was taken from *Also Sprach Zarathustra*, a tone poem by Richard Strauss, which is based on a work by Friedrich Nietzsche that portrays the struggle of a mortal man to become a godlike superman.

August 16, 1977—the day of Elvis's "death"—adds up to 2001, following the numerological count: 8 (August is the eighth month of the year) +16 (the day of the month) + 1977 (the calendar year) = 2001.

Also totaling 2001 is the day Elvis was born (8), plus the day he died (16), plus his age in years at death (42), plus the year of his birth (1935).

What's more, when you consider the full date of August 16, 1977 (or 8 + 16 + 1977 = 2001), another interesting reading is possible: 2001 can also be read without its zeros, giving us a reading of 21. In *Cheiro's*, the number 21 is symbolized by the picture of "the universe" and it is also called the Crown of the Magi. (Elvis was often referred to as "the king.") Twenty-one is a number of advancement, honors, elevation in life. It also means victory after a long fight. The Crown of the Magi is only gained after long initiation and numerous tests of determination. Twenty-one is a fortunate number of promise if it appears in any connection with future events.

Also: 2001, from another particular numerological perspective, is 2 + 1 = 3. The number three represents the power of the Pyramid and of the Trinity.

It's interesting to note that Lisa's wedding date (to Danny Keough) was October 3, 1988, which also equals 2001.

With regard to Elvis Presley: August 16, 1977, was one of Elvis's most favorable days. If any new plans were to be made, this was the best day to put them into action.

Let's take the number sixteen, the day Elvis left: In *Cheiro's* the number 16 is pictured by a tower struck by lightning from which a man is falling with a crown on his head (the concept of "crown" again). This number is also called the Shattered Citadel. It gives warning of a strange fatality awaiting. If sixteen appears as a compound number relating to the future, it should be carefully noted so that plans can be made in advance in order to avert its fatalistic tendency. In other words: We are not ruled by the numbers in the sense of predestination. We are always the captains of our souls, the masters of our fate. We are not prisoners of the universe and, as certain influences occur, our vibrations can change. Another way to put it: We can "flow with the tide."

Take the number eight (keyed to the month of August): According to *Cheiro's*, number-eight persons belong to a more fatalistic law of vibrations than most. To change from an unlucky number to a more fortunate one, you use the Zodiac period just opposite your own, which in this case would be "the house of the moon," or the number seven. Take the full name as it is spelled on the grave at Graceland (Elvis Aaron Presley—the double-A version) and you come up with the compound number of twenty-five (25). Add the 2 and the 5 and you get the number 7, which most often portends good fortune or a lucky period.

Pure accident, or numerical planning?

In the context of numerology, August 16, 1977—the number eight together with 2001—signifies the most powerful date possible in the life of Elvis Presley. No other combination of numbers could possibly hold such power for this entertainer.

One cannot discuss Elvis and numerology without discussing astrology, the influence of the stars and planets on human affairs. The following letter from "the king himself" is on display at the Million Dollar Museum in Memphis. Elvis entitles it simply, "Astrology":

LETTER BY ELVIS PRESLEY:
Astrology

It is designed so as to expose the ultimate in height and depth. To relate the strength and weaknesses of those who are willing to accept and are seeking a closer relationship with the Divine. In order to recognize and correct one's faults and be in step. To be capable of understanding the necessity of the changing times. To participate, to create, to express, to appreciate, and to more fully understand his individual role in reaching the divine God. For man to more fully understand and to determine his own destiny. The realization that God is life itself. Upon being able to accept one's faults and weaknesses. To correct them in order to have a better understanding and to be capable of giving love and help to other human beings regardless of color or creed. To appreciate all people. The breaking down of barriers and recognizing individual traits. To be sincere in having the desire to show gratitude and appreciation for that which each individual has given to the world. You create a better understanding for yourself of life and the part you yourself and others play in this world. You are soon recognizing a brighter light within yourself. The sharing of that light with others and feeling the importance of stressing and/or distributing the love and will of God. For Christ, who gave life and hope and faith to the millions of people who have accepted his sacrifice and ray of life. He taught the love of God and the importance for the love of one another by keeping always the importance of expressing gratitude and respect for the greatest miracle of all—life itself!

Fully realizing this particular chapter might open me up to ridicule, I am reminded of the truth that people often mock that which they do not understand. I view it as ignorant not to use all the universe offers when one makes decisions that could indeed affect not only the universe but also one's personal life.

Are we any less affected by the moon than are the waters? We are part of the universe and it is part of us. The universe works by a numerical calendar, and so do we. What we don't understand, but what our universe instinctively understands, is how it all works.

Historians prove that many of our U.S. presidents used numerology and astrology as guides. Great philosophers and thinkers have used these tools as well. I have no doubt there is proof that the moon affects humankind. Remember: moon = luna, and as for what luna + tic gives you, ask any physician or policeman about the full moon and hemorrhaging and crime. This alone should make one think, and encourage one to investigate the possibilities.

On August 16 through August 17, 1987, the Harmonic Convergence took place. When we analyze the date numerologically, we see another eight. On this date people all over the world celebrated the Coming of the New Age, for the Harmonic Convergence was viewed as the threshold of the new millennium, which, it is said, will usher in a thousand years of peace.

Another fan wrote the following letter considering numerology in Elvis's world: "…one more thing that I found interesting was the explanation for the number twenty—the name number of Priscilla Presley. Priscilla states in her book that at the funeral she placed a bracelet on Elvis's wrist depicting a mother and a child with their hands clasped. (This number is called the Awakening—also the Judgment. It is symbolized by the figure of a winged angel sounding a trumpet while from below a man, woman, and child are seen rising from a tomb with their hands clasped in prayer.)"

Since numerology is the universe's planned design of events, and because Elvis was tied to the cosmos via his singing (music being regarded as the language of the universe), would Elvis have left other clues via his music, such as clues keyed to numbers or containing other numerological references? Elvis often complained that people never listened to him, never listened to the lyrics of his songs. Many have made mention of the song (Elvis's last number-one single) "Way Down" from the *Moody Blue* album, which was recorded at Graceland toward the "end." The credits on the record label list Elvis Presley as executive producer.

Many have puzzled over the number AFL1-2428 on the back of the *Moody Blue* album. The first number (1) refers to the cut; the second (2) to the side. "Does the 42 and 8 signify 42 years of age, 8th month?" one fan asked. However, it was Elvis's change of the original lyrics of "Way Down," written by L. Martine, to "Fate is growing closer, and look at my resistance, found lying on the floor, taking me to places that I've never been before" that raised eyebrows. When asked about these changes, Elvis replied, "Man, it just sounds better…"

The question was posed because it brings to mind that Elvis's body was found lying on the floor. This may simply be a stretch of the imagination. On the other hand, perhaps not.

While on the subject of music: Elvis has been called a musical messiah. Those who believe Elvis to be alive—and there are many—declare Elvis will eventually resurface as a spiritual leader, that it was Elvis's deep spirituality that made him fake his death so that he would have the time and freedom to look deep within himself. The pulpit, they believe, will be Elvis's new stage, from which he will lead a religious revival, teaching truths he has learned, his magnetism drawing millions to him and bringing them closer to God.

To this end, in 1990, a non-Elvis song, "Black Velvet," hit the charts, one version recorded by Alannah Myles, the second version by Robin Lee, both of Atlantic Records, both versions focusing on Elvis Presley and "a new religion that will bring you to your knees." The song's lyrics in part declare: "Up in Memphis the music's like a heat wave…'Love Me Tender' leaves 'em crying in the aisles. The way he moved, it was sin…" The Robin Lee video version ends with a shot of Graceland, with boulderlike stones proclaiming, "Elvis lives" and "Elvis is alive."

"Is this song a clue that someone believes Elvis will return?" one fan wrote. "And since Graceland was once a church…?"

It does give one something to think about, particularly in light of the 1989 Graceland purchase of the Graceland Christian Church, located north of the mansion on 4.2 acres. However, because of my own research regarding Elvis's involvement with law enforcement and Operation Fountain Pen, I believe this spiritual side of Elvis, strong as it is, by no means tells the entire story. Decisions of this magnitude—such as deciding to fake one's death—by their very nature are based on more than one element.

There's no doubt that Elvis Presley gave off the most amazing vibrations, especially when onstage and singing. In a 1988 television interview with Brian Corelone, director of the Institute of Parapsychology in Las Vegas, host Billy Goodman asked Mr. Corelone about Elvis, since Corelone had met Elvis personally.

Corelone responded: "I've never felt…such dynamic vibrations…I had once heard somebody say that if Elvis Presley had ever really let go of everything that he had within him, there wouldn't have been billboards big enough or lights bright enough." Corelone said Elvis's vibrations were so intense you would never forget them.

When asked about his visit to Graceland and Elvis's grave, Corelone gave this description: "When we went past the gravesite, I felt absolutely nothing. Part of my training in parapsychology was being taken through cemeteries. My teacher at the time was Richard King, and he'd point to a grave and say, 'Tell me about the person buried here.' He did this with maybe three to five hundred graves. One time he said, 'Tell me what you feel from this one.' I felt nothing. As it turned out, it was a mock grave that had been used for a movie that had been filmed there, and there was never anybody buried there. I felt that same nothingness from Elvis's grave."

Goodman then asked: "The vibrations you felt when he was alive would have been there with the body dead, as a dead body?"

"The characteristics of the vibrations would have been the same. But the intensity would have been far less."

"And they were not there?"

"No."

On a personal level I have no problem accepting that Elvis was and will always be a special light in the universe—a gift from God. I've long accepted that there is a part of God in all of us. In truth, back in 1977 when I wrote the novel *Orion* (about a superstar who fakes death—a book that mysteriously disappeared from bookshelves), I felt what Elvis must have suffered. In the following extract from that fictional work, young Orion and his childhood friend Tuck discuss their place in the universe. Here Orion first voices his desire to be something special, like the sun. When Tuck reminds him the sun is just a star, Orion replies:

"But it's not 'just a star,' Tuck! That's what I am trying to tell you. The sun is the king of stars. It's the grandest star of all, and its light is brighter and warmer…"

Tuck tried to comprehend what Orion was attempting to explain but his meaning was elusive. "So?"

"So if a star burns out nobody much cares because there are so many more million stars burning and there are more being born. But if the sun burns out, well then, everybody notices. Even in an eclipse, when the sun is only black for a moment, people take notice and they worry. If the sun would die the whole universe would mourn." Orion lowered his eyes, pondering what he had said. Never had he become so deeply involved with life nor so anguished, and even though he was only ten a sense of time and death took hold, a panic-stricken feeling that he was in a race with life itself.

More and more puzzled, Tuck said, "I don't know whether I would want that kind of responsibility. When the sun sets everyone expects it to rise in the morning. That's an awful responsibility, an awful lonely burden." Tuck shook his head. "No, Orion, if that's what you mean by being 'something special,' I wouldn't want no part of it. I'd rather be out there with all the other stars in the universe, shining when I want to shine, resting when I want to rest, with nobody expecting nothing of me."

Orion flushed with embarrassment. Who was he anyway to even dream of being the sun, the king of stars? He was as common as the moss he sat on. Reaching for the picnic basket, Orion wondered why his mama was constantly telling him, "Someday you'll be something special, Orion Eckley Darnell. You was born for it as sure as the sun rises and sets. God told me you was 'special' and you'll see—someday, you'll see."

Handing Tuck a slice of corn bread and a piece of sausage, Orion murmured, "I think every man should at least try to be the sun, even for a day, just to see what it's like."

Tuck broke off a corner of the bread and began chewing slowly. Orion was strange and complicated at times, but as Tuck looked at his friend's face, he now found it totally uncomplicated and serene. For a fleeting moment a thought took hold of Tuck: Was it possible to be the king of stars for a day, and then return to being a common light in the universe?

This is a question worth repeating in the present tense: Is it possible to be the king of stars for a day, and then return to being a common light in the universe?

***

The novel *Orion* was published by Simon & Schuster/Pocket Books, New York, August, 1981 and in another edition by Tudor Publishing, New York, 1989. Because of demand, we hope to see *Orion* republished, especially in light of its shocking history.

6

CLUES

If Elvis left clues to his acts and their meanings, and I believe he did, another major clue is on display at Graceland's museum, where some of Elvis's favorite books can be seen. One book that captures attention immediately is *The Passover Plot* by Hugh Schonfield (New York: Bernard Geis, 1966)—a book detailing how Jesus hoaxed his own death.

Elvis reportedly said he liked this book in that it described step by step that Jesus was no milk-and-water Messiah but rather one who was master of his own destiny, including his "death." Realizing how connected Elvis felt toward Jesus—meaning Elvis's desire to live and do as Jesus taught—*The Passover Plot* is definitely worthy of examination. As with all his favorite books, Elvis read *The Passover Plot* many times over. Perhaps he saw something of himself in every page despite the fact that the book is written about the life of Jesus, not about Elvis. Although I read *The Passover Plot* when it first came out, until after Elvis died I had not focused on how startling the similarities are between the life of Jesus and the life of Elvis— especially when one attempts to read *The Passover Plot* through Elvis's eyes.

Others besides me, including Mitchell Fink, formerly with the Los Angeles *Herald Examiner,* have noted the possibility of Elvis's using *The Passover Plot* as a spiritual road map for what he did: hoax his death. In light of widespread thought on this very topic, let's take a look at what others have surmised.

An extract from a letter by Fern B., of Mentor, Ohio:

A man looking for reasons for who he was and why he was put on this earth to be what he had become might feel that the answers to all his questions could be found in the Bible and other books. We find in [Jesus] the symbol both of martyrdom and the aspirations of man, and therefore we must cling to him as the embodiment of an assurance that our life has meaning and a purpose. I believe that after reading *The Passover Plot*, it could plant in some people's minds a way of removing themselves without actually removing themselves at all.

The perfect plan!

I found the dates of Jesus's crucifixion similar to those of Elvis's death, and the time of Jesus's death and His Resurrection similar to the time that some say Elvis died and when he was found. And to read that Jesus had been taken to the Garden of Gethsemane after his death caught my attention. Naturally, Elvis read this…so now all close family members are buried in Graceland's Meditation Gardens.

Schonfield states that Jesus would have used only close friends (a few) and family to help him fake his own death, like the Beloved Disciple. (Who was he? Not even the Bible tells us. Was Dr. Nick Elvis's Beloved Disciple?)

No one reading *The Passover Plot* cannot ask that maybe Jesus used drugs to make himself look dead—for someone looking for answers, as Elvis was, this would have helped in his plan for death: to cheat death, to give the appearance of death.

Jesus stayed in the public eye before his death, as did Elvis.

[According to Schonfield], if Jesus was alive, who could tell how or when he would appear, what he would look like. Had not Elijah been revealed in the guise of John the Baptist? (Did Elvis, after reading these same words, use

the name John [or Jon] Burrows because it was done in
the Bible? The word "burrow" means to hide [oneself] in
a burrow or a place of refuge. Strange!)

Another correspondent pointed out ways the writer of *The
Passover Plot* keyed the novel to themes that also run through Elvis's
own life. Though *The Passover Plot* was originally written about
Jesus, the following observations about the story's lead character fit
Elvis almost exactly—sometimes amazingly so. Thus one can
appreciate why Elvis held this book in such high esteem:

1. This child was to prove to be no ordinary boy, for he was
   destined to play a unique part in history. This is how we must
   understand him as the one above all others who showed
   mankind how to make their dreams come true.
2. His disciples became familiar with his spells of silence, which
   they feared to break. They would be walking with him,
   talking animatedly among themselves, even arguing heatedly,
   virtually ignoring his presence. Suddenly he would say
   something, either at the time or later, which showed that he
   was not wholly inattentive and had heard their conversation.
3. He says and does things quite unexpected by his intimate
   associates, which takes them by surprise or which they are
   unable to fathom. They may like to think they are wholly in
   his confidence, and even that he will do what they have in
   mind for him. But he baffles and defeats them, and makes
   arrangements of which they have not been cognizant, to
   secure his objectives.
4. The effect of all he may have endured as he contemplated
   what was to come, and dared not betray his secret, were
   bound to take their toll and show themselves in his physical
   appearance.
5. Rapidly, his fame spread far and wide, and his name became
   a legend overnight. Nothing was too impossible to be
   credited to him. There were those, on the other hand, who
   were scandalized by his teaching and behavior, particularly

members of the Pharisee fraternity, who considered themselves to be the custodians of the nation's moral and spiritual instruction. The more straitlaced of them winced at some of the things he said and were offended by the freedom of his conduct. Like a man who has experienced what is called conversion, he felt in himself that he was a new being, and this feeling would have been stimulated by his sudden emancipation from the tension engendered by the long years of waiting, by the knowledge that he had liberty to speak and act now instead of having everything pent up inside him.

6. Jesus had now to prepare for the most difficult and dangerous part of his present mission, which demanded the utmost caution and the most careful organization and timing. He could not look to his disciples to assist him directly in the arrangements for his coming ordeal.

7. He dies about 3:00 PM [at about age forty-one].

8. Two things, however, were indispensable to the success of a rescue operation. The first was to administer a drug to give the impression of premature death, and the second was the speedy delivery of the body to Joseph. [Could "Joseph" equate to "Joe" Esposito?]

9. If he were to cheat death, it was essential that, well in advance of the time, he would have to give every appearance of being dead. Further, help must speedily be forthcoming. Unless his body came into possession of friendly hands, there would be no possibility of his recovery—we would have to imagine how Jesus contrived to give the impression of death, and suggest a way in which his body could have been secured by his friends. We have only to allow that in this, as in other instances, Jesus made private arrangements with someone he could trust, who would be in a position to accomplish his design.

10. When stripped of supernaturalism, the empty tomb may point rather to a removal of the body from the place where the women had seen it laid and its burial elsewhere. But if the body of Jesus had been taken from the tomb by his friends on

Saturday night, we would be ready to agree with the Gospels that the immediate disciples of Jesus knew nothing about this, and they would be quite sincere in indignantly repudiating any contention that they had been guilty of perpetuating a fraud [the hoaxing of a death].

11. If Jesus was alive, who could tell how and when he would appear, what he would look like?

12. Again, an important ingredient is the failure to identify Jesus—this time by his own relatives.

13. Neither had there been any fraud on the part of Jesus himself. He had schemed in faith for his physical recovery.

14. When the few saw him, they were in awe; but some doubted.

15. The special conditions that produced him at a peculiar and pregnant moment in history are never likely to occur again.

Substitute Elvis's name in numbers 1 through 15 and you'll see how uncanny *The Passover Plot* is with regard to a possible faked-death scenario as part of a plot involving Elvis Presley.

Audrey N., another letter writer, did just that when she substituted Elvis's name in place of Jesus in the hardback edition of *The Passover Plot*. In order that the reader might be able to reference her comments, page numbers have been provided:

1. Elvis made private arrangements with someone he could trust, who would be in a position to accomplish this design. (p. 163)

2. Was this person a member of the family or a friend? After the task, this person disappears completely from view. Afterward, there is no indication of associating with Elvis. Elvis plotted and schemed with utmost skill, making secret arrangements, taking advantage of every circumstance conducive to the attainment of his objectives. It is difficult to credit that he had neglected to do anything about the supreme crisis of his career, when it was imperative that he should outwit the forces arrayed against him and wrest victory from the very jaws of death. (p. 163)

3. Elvis would have to give every appearance of being dead. Further help must speedily be forthcoming. Unless his body came into possession of friendly hands, there would be no possibility of his recovery. Elvis contrived to give the impression of death, and the circumstances suggest a way in which his body could have been secured by his friend. (p. 163)

4. Considerations of safety and secrecy will have dictated that as few people as possible should be in the know or involved, and these would not have included any of the disciples [Elvis's Memphis mafia were termed his disciples], in whom he never confided his plans. His was the mastermind, and the ones to whom he gave his instructions neither worked together nor were acquainted with more than their specific function. (pp. 166-167)

5. The disciples [Memphis mafia] knew nothing and would be quite sincere in indignantly repudiating any contention that they had been guilty of perpetuating a fraud. (p. 172)

6. Elvis may not have overlooked that he might taste death in spite of the measure he had secretly taken for his survival. He knew, however, that his followers [fans?] would be in anguish. (p. 173)

7. Some rushed to tell of having seen Elvis. Another ingredient was added to the myth. (p. 176)

8. If Elvis is alive, who could tell how or when or where he would appear, or what he would look like? Cheered by the strange discourses, the followers [fans] were soon telling each other that the man seen must be Elvis. (p. 177)

9. When the few saw him, they were in awe, but some doubted. (p. 179)

10. Neither had there been any fraud on the part of Elvis himself. He had schemed in faith for his physical recovery. (p. 168)

11. The special conditions that produced him at a peculiar and pregnant moment in history are never likely to occur again. (p. 181)

Keep in mind that the passages above, as originally written, were meant to depict Jesus, not Elvis. Yet the book's descriptions of a man much like Elvis might explain why *The Passover Plot* was one of Elvis's favorite books—and a book he left behind (recall *Cheiro's Book of Numbers* and the Bible were missing from Elvis's nightstand), perhaps to be prominently displayed at the Graceland museum. Another of Elvis's enigmatic clues? The parallels seem too mindboggling to be chalked up to sheer coincidence.

What I found equally mindboggling were the sheer number of letters I received regarding Elvis and *The Passover Plot* and how similar many of the analyses have been. The consistent themes and sequences of events the writers discuss demonstrate how strong the observable parallels are between the personal character of the Jesus of Schonfield's novel and the real-life Elvis; likewise, knowing Elvis's familiarity with *The Passover Plot*, the parallels between the death hoax depicted in the novel and methods Elvis may very well have used in his own death hoax are too conspicuous to be overlooked.

Another extract, from Joan G. of Portage, Indiana:

> ...the destined road led to torture—but these things had to come about in the manner predicted and after preliminaries entailing the most careful scheming and plotting to produce them. *Moves and situations had to be anticipated, rulers and associates had to perform their functions without realizing that they were being used.* [Italics are Joan G.'s]
>
> Two things, however, were indispensable to the success of a rescue operation. First, administer a drug to give the impression of a premature death and, second, obtaining the speedy delivery of the body [to someone who was in on the plot. Here Joan is paraphrasing the book. (p. 166)]

From Marcella B., of Belleville, Illinois:

"In *The Passover Plot*, I find most interesting the following passages: '...people struggling frantically to reach Him, to touch even the sacred fringe of His robe as He passed...by the end of most days He was utterly exhausted...He could not get away and He himself saw to it that He would not be forgotten, that He would be continually pestering and challenging us. In spite of everything done to stop Him in His own time and since…He has continued to come through.'"

A survey of the hundreds of letters that have come to me regarding this particular topic underscores the essential point: The book's many correlations between the life of Jesus and Elvis's own life—a likeness in personal style and professional aims Elvis must certainly have noted when delving into *The Passover Plot*.

Faye H. of Tulsa, Oklahoma wrote: "I have read and studied *The Passover Plot* and find it very interesting. One thing I found fascinating and almost a dead giveaway was the 'shedding of white clothes and leaving them neatly folded in the tomb.'

"When did anyone ever change clothes on a corpse[?], yet on page 439 of the paperback *Elvis: We Love You Tender* [by Dee Presley and the Stanleys (New York: Dell Publishers, 1979)], Dee Presley (who was married to Elvis's father Vernon) described Elvis as dressed in a white suit looking 'frighteningly different.' Then on page 440 she says he was changed into a pale blue suit…"

Or as another writer observed, "Was the changing of the clothes symbolic of the changing of Jesus's death robes?"

The above letters are only a sampling of the letters I have received concerning Elvis and *The Passover Plot*. Moreover, a very tattered paperback copy of a January 1977 edition of *The Passover Plot* arrived in the mail. There was no note, no reference as to who sent it, and because of the amount of mail, clippings, books, and so forth coming into this office, the best I can do is say the envelope may have had an Ohio postmark. Because I did not at first fully comprehend the significance behind the arrival of this book, the envelope initially went into the trash can with other envelopes. I had to rummage around in order to find the one I believed the book arrived in. The book's significance lay in some of its underlined passages, such as the following (with parenthetical commentaries by me):

· "The root of Jesse." (Elvis's twin was Jesse, his root.)
· Jesus's death at around age 41 or under 50. (Elvis's "death" was at age 42.)

- Free the mind of preconceived ideas.
- Destroy an illusion and the man behind the myth.
- King of the line of David. (Elvis felt he was from this line—the city of Nashville lies in Tennessee's Davidson County.)
- Jesus was taunted with being a demon-possessed Samaritan. (Elvis, although generous, was also charged with being the devil in disguise.)
- A call to office.
- Killed and be raised again the third day.
- Jesus was the eldest of a fairly large family and brought up in humble circumstances. (Although Elvis was an only child, he came from a large extended family whom he helped support.)
- He saw himself acting out prophecies.
- It was from the banks of Jordan that Elijah had been taken up to Heaven, and now in the guise of John, as it could be thought, he had come back as foretold. (Elvis's "other name" is John and/or Jon Burrows.)
- Jesus and his psychic experiences.

Recall that in the Bible (as well as in *The Passover Plot*) Jesus's tomb was found empty except for the shroud. This takes on a certain significance in light of Larry Geller's statement in his book that Elvis asked that Larry bring to him the book *The Shroud of Turin* (this was most likely a translation of a German-language book about the Shroud, published by Werner Bulst, since Doubleday's American version of Ian Wilson's *Shroud* was not released until 1978). According to close friends and family, it appeared that "Elvis was expecting to find something in its reading." This was the last book found beside Elvis's "body"—a book concerning a shroud bearing what is thought to be the image of Jesus—an image thought to be the result of a cosmic force "that brought Jesus back to life."

It's interesting to note that books about the Shroud of Turin relate to imagery, or even the thought that "seeing is not necessarily believing."

Other scholars and experts think the shroud is a hoax.

Was this, too, another clue?

If clues were left by Elvis, certainly *The Passover Plot* is a major one. However, there are a few other Elvis books that are also on display at Graceland and/or known to be favorites of Elvis:

The King by Morton Cooper (New York: Bernard Geis, 1967). This novel's story is about a forty-four-year-old singer named Orlando, who is "the King." In order to redirect his way of life, he decides to work in the President's administration.

- Orlando has charisma, talent—and the public adores him.
- There is a Madison Square Garden performance that is to be Orlando's last and is telecast by CBS.
- Orlando studies medical books when he cannot sleep.
- He has a longtime friend who is a doctor.
- He has become friends with the President of the United States.
- He acts in movies.
- He is divorced but still loves his first wife.
- He gives generously—and anonymously—to the needy, the sick, and to charities.
- His stage presence is overpowering.

The jacket blurb for *The King* reads: "In the posh Manhattan hotel suite of President Joseph Haywood, Orlando brushed off the fawning hangers-on and left for Madison Square Garden. And as he sang, he said a silent good-bye to it all, because he decided to get off the dizzy merry-go-round of his life, to trade it all for a job in President Haywood's administration…[It would give him] a last chance to do something that would make him proud to look the world in the eye."

Bringes Ans Licht (no author is listed). First published by a German-based company (the German title means "Bring It to Light" or "Reveal It"); released in England under the title *Fairytale* (Derbyshire, U.K.: Heanor Record Center Ltd., 1985). This novel portrays a performer who plans a fake death.

- *Fairytale* is the story of a rock star named Aaron Wade whose "death" is questionable.

· *Fairytale* has a Joe Esposito-like character who, with Aaron, is planning the "death."

· Book concludes with a "to be continued" type of ending.

Fans who have read *Fairytale* have pointed out that the book's title is also the title of a song, one of Elvis's favorites. The song is in effect the story of a man who packs up his things and walks away, feeling that his life would only get worse if he stayed, saying his life is only a dream, a fairytale. The color of the book is blue, Elvis's favorite color. The name "Aaron Wade" is significant in itself and may have broader ramifications: "Aaron," of course, has an obvious connection as a variant of Elvis's middle name. Further, Elvis played a character named Jess Wade in his favorite movie, *Charro*, a non-singing role. In addition, Jess resembles the name of Elvis's dead twin, Jesse.

***

Other books that Elvis read that might be worth studying, not only for clues regarding the "death" of Elvis, but also to get a better insight into his spiritual nature. Among these are:

The Impersonal Life by Joseph Benner (Marina Del Rey, CA: Devorss & Company, 1941).

The Prophet by Kahlil Gibran (New York: Alfred Knopf, 1923).

The Initiate by Cyril Scott (York Beach, ME: Samuel Weiser, Inc., 1920).

Autobiography of a Yogi by Paramahansa Yogananda (Self-Realization, 1974).

The Elvis – Jesus Mystery by Cindy Godfrey (Revelations Publishing, PO Box 1125, New Philadelphia, Ohio 44663)[*Note: Although Elvis didn't read it, it's worth noting for similarities.*]

Rather than dissect these books, I've included various comments in the following chapter, which deals with Elvis's spiritual beliefs. Perhaps the following notation that appears in Elvis's own hand in many of his spiritualistic books says it best: "Should I return, you would not recognize me."

7
PRESENCE

There should be little doubt by now how important a role spirituality played in Elvis Presley's life. One of those who knew this to be true is Larry Geller, Elvis's friend and spiritual advisor. For a more in-depth study regarding this subject I highly recommend the reading of Mr. Geller's book *If I Can Dream: Elvis' Own Story*, written with Joel Spector and Patricia Ramanowski (New York: Simon & Schuster, 1989).

Points elaborated upon by Mr. Geller (and others) include:

- Elvis had a desert vision where he saw himself as the Christ. (Keep in mind that Jesus's family name was not "Christ." Christ is an honorific term from Christus (Latin)/Christos (Greek), meaning "appointed one or messiah," which also signifies "anointed one and/or expected king and deliverer of the Jews." In order to ward off charges of blasphemy, understanding Elvis's love for Jesus *as the Christ* is paramount. When Elvis saw God/Christ/Jesus within himself, he was touching on the basic truth taught us: that we are indeed created in the image of our Maker—God.)
- Elvis believed that his true mission was "God and the Brotherhood."
- Elvis said he had given his life over to the Lord, that he had meditated, prayed, asked God how "Elvis" fit into the universal picture.

- Elvis was deeply concerned about people's suffering; he wanted to bring happiness into their lives and believed that his mission in life was to "uplift." He was grateful for his talents, but he was questioning of his position and what further role God intended for him; Elvis felt deeply that God wanted to use him in a bigger way.
- Elvis believed he had a mission. He explained that this mission had to do with a secret spiritual life. He said that changes would occur—soon—for he already felt it was going to happen. He continually asked God to show him the way, to give him strength, to help him find his true mission in life.
- Elvis believed that, when one twin died, the other inherited his qualities.
- Elvis became fascinated with numbers, letters, and symbols as they related to the universe. The universe's systematic order was a source of enlightenment to him.
- Elvis felt that the Bible was full of "hidden meanings," codes, mystical revelations. (**AUTHOR'S NOTE:** If Elvis were to abandon one life for another, it would fall within his psyche to leave clues, codes, and hidden meanings.)
- Elvis discovered that in Judaism rabbis changed people's names according to the principles of numerology. (Could it be that in the name change of Aron to Aaron, the resulting numbers or combination of numbers would better interpret Elvis's character or fate?)
- Elvis, after hearing the explanation of the Hebrew word c'hai, meaning "life," began wearing the character for this symbol (for instance, as a c'hai medallion) around his neck.
- Elvis emphasizes Geller, was one of the brightest, most intelligent of men, devouring books, not simply reading them but absorbing them, writing his thoughts in the margin, underlining—most of the books dealt with spiritual quests, with "opening up" oneself.
- Elvis said he wanted to become a monk and join a monastery. (Doesn't this mean giving one's life to God—"dropping out" —

giving up the material for the spiritual in order to become Christlike?)

- Elvis said he would never allow himself to degenerate into a fifty-year-old entertainer and even said he wouldn't make it much past forty—which he didn't (at least not as an entertainer).
- Elvis was so anxious to attain higher knowledge that he wanted to take shortcuts; he eventually realized there were no instant techniques but rather the requirement of dedication to years of study and practice.
- Elvis loved plans and projects.
- Elvis, especially after Vernon's marriage to Dee fell apart, saw that everything around him was breaking down.
- Elvis said and did things that suggested he might also be making sweeping changes, even planning to make a new start.
- Elvis began talking about going to Europe, even to Japan. (Could it be that as Elvis-the-entertainer he felt that he couldn't see the planet earth without first "leaving it"?—a thought he once shared with a writer with *National Geographic* magazine.)
- Elvis, by April of 1977, said he was on the brink of making major changes in his life.
- Elvis, toward the end of April 1977, talked about a secret spiritual life and a special mission.
- Elvis, by the end of May of that year, talked about something described as "top secret."
- Elvis said he wanted to live a different kind of life, that the one he was living had gone on long enough.
- Elvis told Geller that this different kind of life would begin by the end of the summer, and that, yes, it would happen.

(AUTHOR'S NOTE: There is nothing in Mr. Geller's book and there was nothing personally said to me by Mr. Geller that indicates a belief on his part that Elvis faked his death. In fact, in public interviews, Mr. Geller has said the opposite.)

Less than three months after the April and May talks with Larry

Geller in which Elvis mentioned various (and nonspecific) plans, secrets, missions, and life changes to come, on August 16, 1977, the life Elvis had known did end. Did it end the way the public was told, with Elvis's physical death? Or is it possible it ended the way Elvis—the ultimate planner—had intended? Those familiar with Elvis know that he very well could have done it "his way."

"From the House of David will come the messiah" is a Jewish prophecy. The fact that Nashville—the music capital—is in Davidson County held symbolic significance for Elvis. Around his neck Elvis wore the Star of David along with the Christian cross. According to at least one biographer, Elvis was proud there was Jewish blood on his mother's side of the family, and often made reference to his Hebrew heritage. One genealogist has even traced Elvis's ancestry back to the House of David, which is the same ancestry as Jesus, with whom Elvis identified. So proud was Elvis that his mother had Jewish blood that he had the Star of David placed on her headstone at Forest Hill Cemetery. (This has been discussed earlier in the book in the context of Elvis's fascination with the book *The Passover Plot*.)

There was and is indeed an eerie conjunction between Elvis's life and the life of Jesus—a link that cannot be explained away by suggesting it as simply being one of life's everyday similarities, an intriguing one at that.

Both men were called "the king," although Elvis was quick to say he considered Jesus, rather than himself, the true king. Both Jesus and Elvis had grown far beyond the confines of sectarianism, viewing bigotry as a limit of one's "God-soul," or the God that is in all of us. These two men felt the hellfire-and-brimstone teachings of some churches to be morally wrong. In both men's minds God should be loved, not feared. These shared beliefs ran far deeper than church walls, choirs, or icons. The essence that Elvis called the "God-breath" within his soul wanted to emulate what Jesus taught: love, charity, relief of others' suffering, the abandonment of material trappings, healing and helping. Elvis's belief in reincarnation is well documented, although he was hesitant to speak of this phenomenon around those who possessed a "closed mind."

From the moment Elvis was born there was something "different" about him. Elvis's father, Vernon, spoke of the blue light that shone from the heavens the night Elvis was born: "It was so powerful that the outside of our small house was bathed in this light, while the two inside rooms were a violet color…" (Two of Elvis's favorite colors were blue and violet.)

The moon was also strange the night Elvis was born. The lower half of the moon was darkened, while the upper half poured beams of light down upon the earth. Elvis was born with a birthmark similar to this same shape the moon takes—an occurrence that comes to pass only once a year.

In an article that appeared in *Angel Times* magazine (Atlanta, Georgia), writer Maia C.M. Shamayyim described this birthmark as "a diamond discoloration, bearing a cut-out-upside-down bowl or crescent of normal pigmentation within the upper lefthand corner of the dark diamond, eclipsing the left edge of the birthmark. The mark was on his groin or inner thigh. Interestingly, the wounded thigh is a symbol of several ancient myths and legends, giving various interpretations. One meaning is that of someone appointed for spiritual service whose body is wounded or maimed to release illumination to the people."

There is no doubt that Elvis radiated intense energy and light.

Larry Geller has talked about how, from their first meeting, he knew of Elvis's spiritual quality, that Elvis could silence a room just by the power of his aura. Countless others have described Elvis's "overwhelming power of presence."

Columnist Bob Green wrote in his 1981 review of the *This Is Elvis* docudrama that when Elvis dominated the screen, the audience was silent, almost reverential.

Bernard Benson, author of *The Minstrel* (Memphis, TN: Minstrel Publishing, 1976), to explain Elvis's effect on the world could only comment: "This great force cannot be explained."

Sean Shaver, who was Elvis's official photographer in the 1970s, explains in his book *Elvis: Photographing the King* (Kansas City, MO: Timur Publishing), that no one watching Elvis could ever forget the electric energy flowing back and forth. Many reviewers have stated that, when Elvis came onstage, something extraordinary occurred, something beyond control—magical—something beyond mortal definition, an energy emitted by Elvis alone.

"Elvis looked different to anyone I've ever seen. He was beautiful," said Gordon Stoker, backup for Elvis in the 1950s and 1960s. "He was more alive than anybody I've ever known, more of everything that a human could be."

"He lived his faith," said Kathy Westmoreland, backup singer for Elvis in the 1970s.

Author Dave Marsh commented in his book *Elvis* (New York: Warner Books, 1982) that "Elvis was more than anything a spiritual leader of our generation. There is no way to assess his importance."

Said Patsy Guy Hammontree, author of *Elvis Presley: A Bio-Bibliography*: "In truth the man takes on mythic and archetypal dimensions such that for some fans only Christ is greater."

"Elvis's costumes appeared dull when on a hanger," said one observer. "Yet walking onstage, he and his clothes radiated light. Elvis's aura was so very visible—the Light of his Soul shone through. He was not a closed soul and thus, being so open, was also vulnerable to outside cruelties. Elvis could be hurt so very deeply because he had never built walls, walls which could protect his soul—yet the same walls which would hide the Soul-Light."

Another reaction oft repeated in meeting Elvis: "He was a phenomenon—he was electricity."

Because music is the international language—a language that often bypasses the physical senses—Elvis was able to reach the entire world. Gospel music was his first love and he said, according to the Presley fan magazine *Elvis World*, that he hoped one day he could devote the rest of his life to singing it. Gospel was his foundation stone, and when he sang hymns, his belief became ours, his splendor our splendor.

Dr. W. Herbert Brewster, a Baptist minister, saw this in Elvis: "Like most in the South and in whose soul God has pressed down a harp of a thousand strings, it only needed tuning. Elvis's voice was that kind of voice that agreed with the thought of Calvary."

In March 1979, the late Jeanne Dixon, the noted psychic, wrote:

"It was as if his music opened up a window in the sky through which he could catch a glimpse of the peace denied him here on earth."

Or as Carl Wilson of the Beach Boys musical group said, "His voice was a total miracle."

Many around Elvis said he had the ability to heal. To this end there are countless testimonies by family and friends concerning incidents when Elvis did indeed heal their afflictions. Elvis believed he had this power; he believed in supernatural forces, telepathy, astral projection, and the learning of "the secrets of the Brotherhood." His fascination with Paramahansa Yogananda extended to how the yogi was able to predict "the exact day of his own death." Elvis even visited the Self-Realization Fellowship headed by Sri Daya Mata, a disciple of Paramahansa Yogananda, who gave Elvis secret manuscripts that might help him understand why God had chosen him to be Elvis Presley.

About the remark Elvis voiced during his last concert tour—"I am and I was": Look up the Book of Revelation 1:8: "'I am the Alpha and the Omega,' says the Lord God, who is and who was and who is to come, the Almighty."

The following extract is from a photocopied page of an unnamed religious booklet I received, sent anonymously, a statement that expresses somewhat the same slant as the preceding quotation from the Book of Revelation:

> The people of Yahweh always live between memory and hope, between their conviction that God has acted in the past and their assurance of God's redemptive presence in their future. Just as earthly life had a beginning, so will it have an ending; and Yahweh whose name means "I Am," presides over both. The Being One is most fully revealed in the One "who is and who was and who is to come…"

"I am and I was"—words spoken by Elvis at "the end" of his life as a musical performer—are better understood by the reading of another of Elvis's favorite books, Joseph Benner's *The Impersonal Life*, the first chapter of which is entitled "I Am." A few pages later appears the "Always Was" idea. I recommend reading this book several times for full understanding. Basically, the topic taken up is about the God-power in us, the God-power always in us. We were, are, and always have been—a philosophy Jesus taught, yet one not widely nor often well understood. This God-awareness also translates to: "A man is as he thinks."

As you've noted from the descriptions by others regarding Elvis-the-man and Elvis-the-singer, this entertainer is often described in religious terms. Many have written how Elvis turned their lives from ones of negative actions to ones of positive deeds, that Elvis's presence made them feel "closer to God."

Elvis's daughter Lisa Marie also spoke of her father in glowing terms: "There was an intense feeling to have him around...he was a very powerful person, spiritually."

From the mouth of a child whose hero was: "Elvis Pwesley—he's an angel and is going to take care of the world."

Several philosophers have written with the view that Elvis's soul was a follower of Jesus Christ in that Elvis exuded a presence, a goodness, and an inner knowledge of the suffering of humanity—and the pain of Calvary. Elvis Presley possessed tremendous insight; he gave unconditional love, not only with physical or material gifts, but also by the giving of "self."

There is a family story concerning Elvis as a little boy. He had wanted a tricycle for Christmas. His parents worked overtime in order to get the money. Christmas morning arrived and Elvis was elated. He took his tricycle out to ride, but soon came back without it. His mother questioned him, and Elvis said he had given it away to a little boy who had not gotten anything for Christmas because he was "too poor." Every time Gladys retrieved the tricycle, Elvis again gave it away.

As a boy Elvis told people he saw "beings-of-light," that he talked to them, that they were angels, and that they sang to him. When he told his mother about these experiences she would spank him because she thought he was "devil-possessed." His response was to hug her and tell her it was all right, that she simply didn't understand. In later years he told those he trusted that the beings-of-light he had seen were always with him, telling him, "You are and will always be…"

Elvis believed that our light (soul) comes from the Light of God, but that that light, at one time completely spiritual, was now confined in the physical body—that same light representing the sum total of all knowledge. Belief in and practice in accord with this realization may explain why Elvis seemed to "glow" and why so many millions were and are attracted to this special man—how they automatically love him. Elvis's Jesus-connection obviously embraced the biblical phrase: "I am the way, the truth and the life: no man cometh unto the Father, but by me."

It would take a major treatise to dissect the books that had an effect on Elvis's spiritual life. However, there appears a common thread among them: The message that we are born with the Light of God, and our role is to bring that light forth (God = love). There are masters among us, or those whose God-light is far greater than average. Yet to find one's own mastership, light, soul, it is sometimes necessary to go off from the everyday world to meditate, to study— which can only be accomplished by unshackling oneself from material trappings and removing oneself from those who would mock, condemn—even crucify. When this initiation is complete, a "return is possible."

No one is saying Elvis is or thought he was a god. Elvis was a man, a very special man. However, Elvis did strive to reach "his higher self." He wrote a note that was entitled, "My Vow".

Note from Elvis Presley:
My Vow

I promise to try to live a pure life, to practice faith, to seek perfection, to meditate daily, to practice abstinence and free my body from lusts of the flesh to the best of my ability.

Early in his career, Elvis received a copy of a short essay, "The Penalty of Leadership," written by Theodore F. MacManus. Upon reading this work, Elvis said the author must have been thinking of him when he wrote it, even though it was written before Elvis was born. A framed copy of this essay hung in Elvis's office and is now on display in Graceland's "Sincerely Elvis Museum" along with some of Elvis's favorite books. Elvis is known to have said Theodore F. MacManus's "The Penalty of Leadership" was, in effect, about Elvis's own life:

THE PENALTY OF LEADERSHIP
by
Theodore F. MacManus

In every field of human endeavor, he who is first must perpetually live in the white light of publicity. Whether the leadership be vested in a man or in a manufactured product, emulation and envy are ever at work. In art, in literature, in music, industry, the reward and the punishment are always the same. The reward is widespread recognition; the punishment fierce denial and detraction. When a man's work becomes a standard for the whole world, it also becomes a target for the shafts of the envious few. If his work is merely mediocre, he will be left severely alone—if he achieves a masterpiece, it will set a million tongues a-wagging. Jealousy does not protrude its forked tongue at the artist who produces a commonplace painting.

Whatsoever you write, or paint, or play, or sing, or build, no one will strive to surpass or to slander you, unless your work be stamped with the seal of genius. Long, long after a great work or a good work has been done, those who are disappointed or envious continue to cry out that it cannot be done. Spiteful little voices in the domain of art were raised against Whistler as a mountebank, long after the big world had acclaimed him its great genius. Multitudes flocked to Bayreuth to worship at the shrine of Wagner, while the little group of those whom he had dethroned and displaced argued angrily that he was no musician at all. The little world continued to protest that Fulton could not build a steamboat, while the big world flocked to the river to see his boat steam by. The leader is assailed because he is a leader, and the effort to equal him is merely added proof of that leadership. Failing to equal or to excel, the follower seeks to depreciate and to destroy, but only confirms once more the superiority of that which he strives to supplant. There is nothing new in this.

It is as old as the world and as old as the human passions—envy, fear, greed, ambition, and the desire to surpass. And it all avails nothing. If the leader truly leads, he remains the leader. Master-poet, master-painter, master-workman, each in turn is assailed, and each holds his laurels through the ages. That which is good or great makes itself known, no matter how loud the clamor of denial. That which deserves to live—lives.

***

When, on January 14, 1973, the concert *Elvis: Aloha from Hawaii* was broadcast live on television worldwide and witnessed by an audience of almost two billion, one religious figure noted: "There is a good man…"

ELVIS PRESLEY, DEPUTY SHERIFF.

Page Two (2)

16. Education - Number of years in Elementary __6__ Name of School _EaTUPELO_

     High School _HUMES_____ Graduate _YES_ Date_____

     Tech School or College_____ Name of School_____ Years_____

17. Have you ever been under a doctor's care for a nervous or mental disorder? __No____

     If yes, give name of doctor_____

18. Do you have any handicaps or defects? __No__ If yes, explain fully_____

     _____

19. To what extent do you drink? __DON'T DRINK-_____

20. List three (3) business firms as credit references:

     1._____ Active_____

     2._____ Active_____

     3._____ Active_____

21. Hand Gun Information: Make _S-W_ Model _66_ Caliber _357_____

     Serial Number_____ Blue____ Nickel____ Stainless Steel _X_____

     This weapon owned by_____

     HAND GUN MUST BE APPROVED BY SHERIFF'S DEPARTMENT

PLEASE READ BEFORE SIGNING:

I hereby state that the information entered here
is complete and true to the best of my knowledge.
Any false statement, knowingly or willfully made
will be reason to reject my application. I further agree to abide by the regulations and res-
trictions established governing this commission.
This signature is to authorize a complete background investigation.

Elvis Presley
(Signature)

_11/20/74_
(Date)

A TWENTY-FIVE ($25.00) NON-REFUNDABLE FEE MUST ACCOMPANY THIS APPLICATION IF WEAPON IS CALIBER
.38 SPECIAL. THIRTY-FIVE ($35.00) IF WEAPON IS ANY OTHER CALIBER.

NOTE: If this application is rejected for insufficient references or any other reason, and
the applicant wishes to re-submit, an additional charge of twenty-five ($25.00) will be require

Information below to be filled in if fees and/or bond are to be paid by other than above named
individual:

                              AGENCY OR COMPANY

Firm Name_____ Address_____

Applicant employed on_____ Position_____
                        (Date)   (Full or part time)
Is applicant to bear sidearms while on duty?_____If yes, is this sidearm company owned?_____

Individual_____

Is employer or individual paying for commission?_____

BACKGROUND, TRAINING, BOND AND FEES WILL BE COMPLETED BEFORE COMMISSION IS GRANTED.

/pb:Form 3/74

                                   - 2 -

APPLICATION TO SHELBY COUNTY SHERIFF'S DEPARTMENT OF
approval of Elvis' Smith & Wesson .357 handgun.

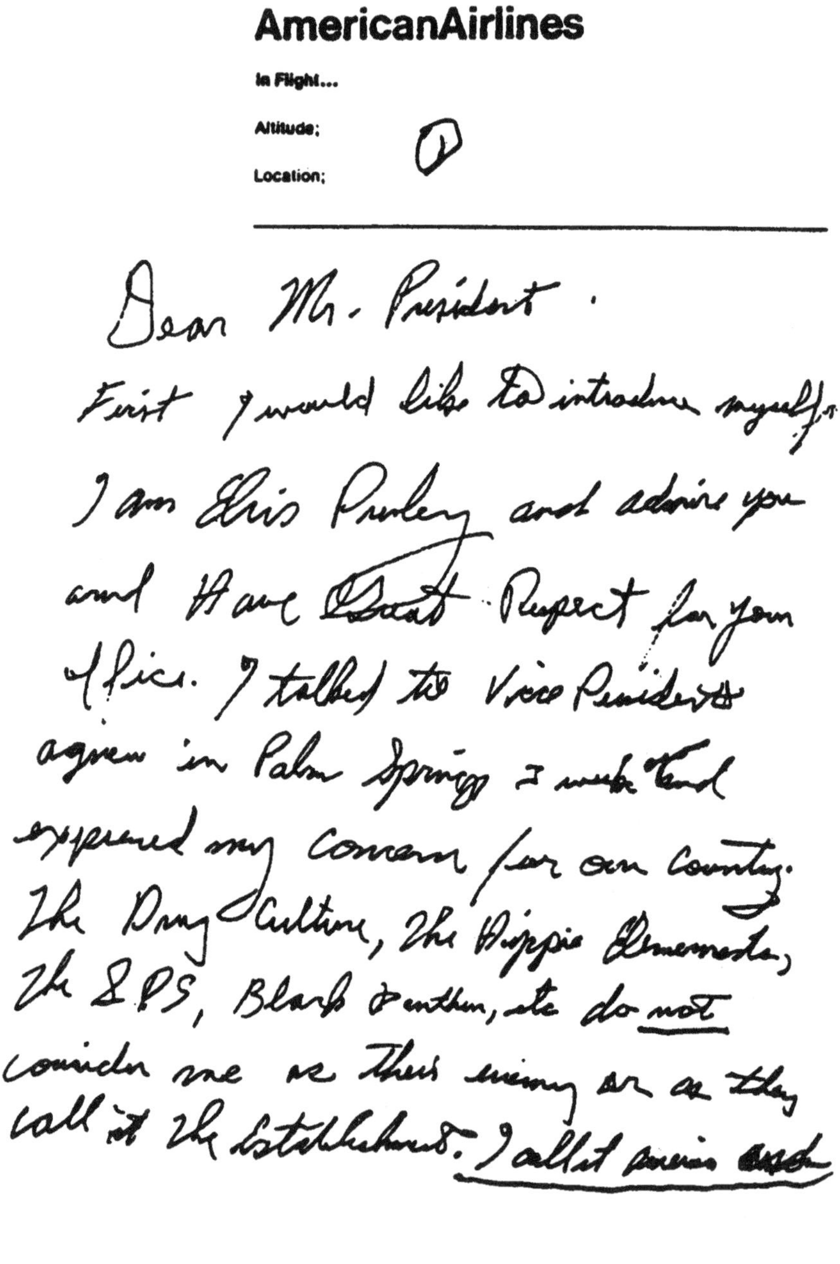

AmericanAirlines

In Flight...

Altitude; ①

Location;

Dear Mr. President.

First I would like to introduce myself. I am Elvis Presley and admire you and Have ~~Great~~ Respect for your office. I talked to Vice President Agnew in Palm Springs 3 weeks ago and expressed my concern for our country. The Drug Culture, The Hippie Elements, The SDS, Black Panthers, etc do not consider me as their enemy or as they call it The Establishment. I call it America and

Elvis' handwritten letter to President Nixon.

AmericanAirlines

In Flight...

Altitude:

Location:

I Love it . Sir I can and will
be of any Service that I can to help
the country out. I have no concern
or motives other than helping the
country out. So I wish not to be
given a title or an appointed position, I can
and will do more good if I were
made a Federal agent at large, and
I will help out by doing it my
way through my communication with people
of all ages. First and Foremost I am an
entertainer but all I need is the Federal
credentials. I am on this Plane with

AmericanAirlines

In Flight...

Altitude;

Location;

③

Sen. George Murphy and We have been discussing the problems that our Country is faced with. So I am Staying at the Washington hotel Room 505-506-507 - I have 2 men who work with me by the name of Jerry Schilling and Sonny West. I am registered under the name of Jon Burrows. I will be here for as long as it takes to get the credentials of a Federal agent. I have done an in depth study of Drug abuse and Communist Brainwashing

AmericanAirlines

In Flight...

Altitude;

Location;   4

Techniques and I am right in the
middle of the whole thing, where
I can and will do the most good
I am Glad to help just so long
as it is kept very Private. You can
have your staff or whomever call
me anytime today, tonight or Tomorrow
I was nominated this coming year
one of America's Ten most outstanding
young men. That will be in January
18 in my Home Town of Memphis Tenn.
I am sending you this about autobiography
about myself so you can better understand This

AmericanAirlines

In Flight...

Altitude;

Location;   *S*

~~approach~~

approach. I would love to
meet you just to say hello if
you're not to Busy.
                    Respectfully,
                        Elvis Presley

P.S. I believe that your Sire
was one of the Top Ten Outstanding Men
of America also.

I have a personal gift for you also
which I would like to present to you
and you can accept it or I will keep it
for you until you can take it.

MEMORANDUM

THE WHITE HOUSE
WASHINGTON

December 21, 1970

MEMORANDUM FOR: MR. H. R. HALDEMAN

FROM: DWIGHT L. CHAPIN

SUBJECT: Elvis Presley

Attached you will find a letter to the President from Elvis Presley. As you are aware, Presley showed up here this morning and has requested an appointment with the President. He states that he knows the President is very busy, but he would just like to say hello and present the President with a gift.

As you are well aware, Presley was voted one of the ten outstanding young men for next year and this was based upon his work in the field of drugs. The thrust of Presley's letter is that he wants to become a "Federal agent at large" to work against the drug problem by communicating with people of all ages. He says that he is not a member of the establishment and that drug culture types, the hippie elements, the SDS, and the Black Panthers are people with whom he can communicate since he is not part of the establishment.

I suggest that we do the following:

> This morning Bud Krogh will have Mr. Presley in and talk to him about drugs and about what Presley can do. Bud will also check to see if there is some kind of an honorary agent at large or credential of some sort that we can provide for Presley. After Bud has met with Presley, it is recommended that we have Bud bring Presley in during the Open Hour to meet briefly with the President. You know that several people have mentioned over the past few months that Presley is very pro the President. He wants to keep everything private and I think we should honor his request.

I have talked to Bud Korgh about this whole matter, and we both think that it would be wrong to push Presley off on the Vice President since it will take very little of the President's time and it can be extremely beneficial for the President to build some rapport with Presley.

In addition, if the President wants to meet with some bright young people outside of the Government, Presley might be a perfect one to start with.

Approve Presley coming in at end of Open Hour_____

Disapprove_____

WHITE HOUSE MEMORANDUM FROM DWIGHT W. CHAPIN TO H.R. HALDEMAN CONCERNING PRESIDENTIAL MEETING WITH ELVIS PRESLEY.

EXECUTIVE

THE WHITE HOUSE

$H\acute{E}\,5\text{-}1$
$P\!\!\cancel{\mathcal{R}}\,7\text{-}1/P^{+}$

WASHINGTON

December 21, 1970

$A\!\!\!/$

MEMORANDUM FOR: THE PRESIDENT

SUBJECT: Meeting with Elvis Presley
December 21, 1970
12:30 p. m.

I.   PURPOSE

To thank Elvis Presley for his offer to help in trying to stop
the drug epidemic in the country, and to ask him to work with
us in bringing a more positive attitude to young people throughout the country.

In his letter to you, Elvis Presley offered to help as much as
possible with the growing drug problem. He requested the
meeting with you this morning when he presented himself to
the guard at the Northwest Gate bearing a letter.

II.   PARTICIPANTS

Elvis Presley

Bud Krogh (staff)

III.   TALKING POINTS

A. We have asked the entertainment industry - both television
and radio - to assist us in our drug fight.

B. You are aware that the average American family has 4 radio
sets; 98% of the young people between 12 and 17 listen to
radio. Between the time a child is born and he leaves high
school, it is estimated he watches between 15,000 and
20,000 hours of television. That is more time than he spend
in the classroom.

WHITE HOUSE MEMORANDUM FOR THE PRESIDENT FROM BUD KROGH
REGARDING PRESIDENTIAL MEETING WITH ELVIS PRESLEY.

C. The problem is critical: **As of December 14, 1970, 1,022 people died this year in New York alone from just narcotic related deaths. 208 of these were teenagers.**

D. Two of youth's folk heroes, Jimi Hendrix and Janis Joplin, recently died within a period of two weeks reportedly from drug-related causes. Their deaths are a sharp reminder of how the rock music culture has been linked to the drug sub-culture. If our youth are going to emulate the rock music stars, from now on let those stars affirm their conviction that true and lasting talent is the result of self motivation and discipline and not artificial chemical euphoria.

E. Suggestions for Presley activities:

1. Work with White House Staff

2. Cooperate with and encourage the creation of an hour Television Special in which Presley narrates as stars such as himself sing popular songs and interpret them for parents in order to show drug and other anti-establishment themes in rock music.

3. Encourage fellow artists to develop a new rock musical theme, "Get High on Life."

4. Record an album with the theme "Get High on Life!" at the federal narcotic rehabilitation and research facility at Lexington, Kentucky.

5. Be a consultant to the Advertising Council on how to communicate anti-drug messages to youth.

AGENT ELVIS PRESLEY.

PRESIDENT NIXON AND ELVIS PRESLEY IN THE OVAL OFFICE.

OFFICE OF

SHERIFF OF SHELBY COUNTY

COUNTY OF SHELBY, }
State of Tennessee

By virtue of authority of law in me vested, I do hereby *appoint and constitute*........................Elvis.Aron.Presley............................, *a Deputy Sheriff* under me, in and for the said County of Shelby, to do and perform such duties as are prescribed by law.

This *commission* to continue at my will.

Given under my hand, at office, in the Court House, in the City of Memphis, **this the** ....1....................day of............Sept....................19 76....

........................*Gene Barksdale*........................
Sheriff of Shelby County.

STATE OF TENNESSEE, }
County of Shelby

I do solemnly swear that I will support the Constitution of the United States, and the Constitution and Laws of the State of Tennessee; and that I will discharge the duties of the office of DEPUTY SHERIFF OF SHELBY COUNTY, TENNESSEE, to which I have been appointed, and which I am about to assume; and that I have not given, accepted, or knowingly carried a challenge, in writing or otherwise, to any person being a citizen of the State, or aided or abetted therein, since the adoption of the Constitution in 1835 and that I will not be guilty of either of these acts during my continuance in office: So help me God.

Elvis Presley

Sworn to and subscribed before me, this........................*day* of........................19 ......

........................*Clerk.*

........................*D. C.*

GENE BARKSDALE, SHERIFF OF SHELBY COUNTY, TENNESSEE, DEPUTIZES ELVIS PRESLEY.

DOUBLE-A: MEMORIALS AT GRACELAND

SINGLE-A: CERTIFICATE OF LIVE BIRTH.

SINGLE-A: MARRIAGE CERTIFICATE.

A P P L I C A T I O N
SPECIAL DEPUTY
SHELBY COUNTY SHERIFF'S DEPARTMENT

1. Name _PRESLEY___ _ELVIS___ _ARON___ Date _11/20_ 19_74_
　　　　(last)　　　　(first)　　(middle or maiden)

2. Address_3764 ELVIS PRESLEY BLVD_ _MMPHS_, _TENN_ _38116_ Years _16_
　　　　(street)　　　(city)　　　(state)　　(zip)

3. Age _39_ Date of Birth _1/8/35_ Place of Birth _TUPELO, MISS._ Phone ___

4. Height _6'_ Weight _175_ Sex _M_ Race_CAUCAS._ Hair _BLACK_ Eyes _BLUE_

5. Previous Address_____ From_____

6. Business Name_____ Address_____

　 Phone_____ Title_____ From_____

　 Previous Employer_____ From_____ To_____

　 Previous Employer_____ From_____ To_____

7. Are you a citizen of the U.S.? _YES_ Naturalized_____
　　　　　　　　　　　　　　　　　　　　　　(date)

8. How long a resident of Tennessee? _26 YRS._

9. Social Security No._____ Drivers License No._____

10. Give name, complete addresses and zip codes of at least four personal references who have known you for the past five years or more. Do not include relatives.

　　1._____
　　2._____
　　3._____
　　4._____

　 NOTE: If the above references do not reply or the letter is returned by the Post Office your application WILL BE REJECTED for insufficient references. BE SURE ADDRESSES ARE ACCURATE AND COMPLETE.

11. Have you had previous experience with a City, State or Federal law enforcement agency?

　 _____If yes, name of agency_____

　 From_____ To_____

12. Do you have a current commission with any law enforcement agency? _YES_
　 If yes, name of agency _DENVER POLICE DEPT. LT._ + _SHELBY Co. SHERIFFS DEPT_ CHIEF DEPY
　 Issued(_DENVER_) _1974_ (_SHELBY CO._)_11/24/70_ Expires_____

13. Have you had previous experience with an investigative agency or guard service? _No_

14. Have you ever been fingerprinted by a law enforcement agency? _YES_
　 If yes, name of agency _DENVER P.D. + SHELBY Co. SHERRIFF_ Date_____
　 Reason _COMMISSION_

15. Have you ever been arrested for any charge? _No_ If yes --

Date	Offense	City & State	Disposition

SINGLE-A: APPLICATION, SPECIAL DEPUTY, SHELBY COUNTY SHERIFF'S DEPARTMENT.

JESSIE GARON PRESLEY: MEMORIAL PLAQUE AT GRACELAND.

ELVIS ONSTAGE IN THE SUNDIAL SUIT.

BLOWN-UP SECTION OF POOLHOUSE PICTURE.

MUHAMMAD ALI AND ELVIS PRESLEY.

The ME report.

THE ME REPORT.

Paul R. Weast

Master Certified Graphoanalyst
Certified Document Examiner

April 17, 1990

Gail Brewer-Georgio
1416 Lakeshore Circle
Gainesville, Ga. 30501   File No. Q-41390-E

    Re: Medical Examiner's Report on Elvis A. Presley

Dear Ms. Georgio;

Pursuant to your request received April 13, 1990 I have examined
the following:

QUESTIONED

Exhibit Q-1

A photo copy of a report entitled Office Of The County Medical
Examiner, 858 Madison Ave.,Memphis, Tennessee 38103.
    REPORT OF INVESTIGATION BY COUNTY MEDICAL EXAMINER
This is purported to be a copy of the Medical Examiner's report
on the death of Elvis Aron Presley on August 16,1977. All
information is handwritten and purported to have been written
by the Memphis Medical Examiner, Dr. A. Nichopolous. The
signature at the bottom of page one is not readable.

EXEMPLARS

KNOWN HANDWRITING FOR COMPARISON

Exhibit E-1

A photo copy of a handwritten letter on American Airlines
inflight stationery. It is addressed to President Nixon and
consists of six pages. It is not dated. On page five it is
signed Elvis Presley. Page six lists several telephone numbers
and is also signed Elvis Presley.

1919 Coronet Avenue, #68, Anaheim, California 92801 (714) 758-2907 (714) 550-0528

The Paul Weast Report.

page two
File No. Q-41390-E
Gail Brewer-Georgio

Exhibit E-2

A photo copy of a handwritten letter dated 1/17/63. It is addressed Donna and is signed Elvis Presley.

Exhibit E-3

A photo copy of a Bill of Sale of Southern Motors,Inc. No. 2042. Bears handwritten notation and is signed Elvis Presley.

Exhibit E-4

A photo copy of a restaurant guest check signed Elvis Presley and the notation " Tip $3.00"

Exhibit E-5

A photo copy of a thank you note, postmarked Memphis, Tenn. Nov. 16,1973. It is signed Elvis Presley.

Exhibit E-6

A photo copy of hand printed Christmas Gift list for 1965. At the top it is imprinted Elvis Presley.

Exhibit E-7

Photo copies of the face of two checks bearing a corner card reading E.A. Presley 3764 Elvis Presley Blvd.,Memphis, Tenn 38116. They are drawn on National Bank of Commerce. Check number 168 is dated May 14, 1977 and is signed E.A. Presley. Check number 200 is dated Jan. 14, 1972 and is signed E.A. Presley.

Exhibit E-8

A photo copy of a page from Vida's Autograph Analysis Collection. It bears reproductions of Elvis Presley autographs. One at

page three
File No. Q-43390-E
Gail Brewer-Georgio

age 24 in 1959. Next is dated 1956, next 1967 and the last
is 1977 and labeled " only five months prior to his death."

Exhibit "C"

A photo copy of the first page of the Medical Report greatly
enlarged. It has a signature clipped from the Nixon letter
and pasted under the name Elvis Presley Blvd. to illustrate
the close similarity.

I understand that each of these Exemplar documents can be
authenticated as genuine samples of Elvis Presley's handwriting
and signatures.

METHOF OF EXAMINATION

The signatures reading Elvis Presley or E.A. Presley and the
handwriting and handprinting attributed to Elvis Presley have
each been carefully examined by stereo-microscope and by viewing
with transmitted light on a light table. Each has been measured
for the degree of slant, size, spacing, alignment and proportion.
Individual letter forms have been examined and compared.
Transparent photo copies were produced and viewed in a greatly
enlarged state with an overhead projector. Transparent photo
copies were overlaid over each other for comparisons.

RESULTS OF EXAMINATION

The degree of slant, letter size, spacing, alignment and proportion matches on all documents . The numbers and words reading
3764 Elvis Presley Blvd on the Medical Examiner's report match
numbers and signatures on the President Nixon letter. The
name Elvis Presley in the address match several signatures
of Elvis Presley. The word Entertainer on the ME report matches
very closely the same word written by Elvis Presley in the Nixon

page four
File No.Q-41390-E
Gail Brewer-Georgio

letter. Several of the small letters f   match very closely as do two of
the capital letters F .Capital letters B also match.

OPINION

It is my professional opinion as California Courts qualified
examiner of questioned documents that the handwriting on the
questioned Exhibit Q-1, "Report of Investigation By County
Medical Examiner " was probably produced by the same person
who' produced the handwriting on Exemplar Exhibits E-1 through
E-8 and the signatures that read Elvis Presley or E.A. Presley.

Photo copies of all listed documents are attached to this
report an incorporated herein. Documents supplied to me for
examination are hereby returned to Gail Brewer-Georgio.

Thank you for the opportunity to be of service in this matter.
If I can be of any further service please call on me.

Respectfully submitted,

Paul R. Weast, MGA,CDE
Master Graphoanalyst
Certified Document Examiner

PRW/ bl

Encl: As cited

ROUTINE

CLEAR   **12/30/77** b7C

FM DIRECTOR (87-143603)   2 ████████

TO MIAMI (196-68) ROUTINE

NEW YORK (196-66) ROUTINE

MEMPHIS (196-23) ROUTINE   *NAM FREDERICK PETER PRO*

BT

CLEAR

FREDERICK M. PRO; ET AL; ELVIS A. PRESLEY (DECEASED) - VICTIM;

ITSP; FBW; MF; CONSPIRACY; 00: MEMPHIS.

REBUTELCAL TO MIAMI, DECEMBER 14, 1977.

THIS IS TO CONFIRM REBUTELCAL IN WHICH AUTHORITY WAS b7C

GRANTED FOR SA ████████ TO TRAVEL FROM NEW YORK TO

MIAMI TO CONDUCT INTERVIEW OF ████████ b7D

BT

WASHINGTON HOTEL) PHONE ME 85900
Rm 505-506.
PRIVATE
AND CONFIDENTIAL
UNDER THE NAME
OF JON BURROWS
Atten. President Nixon
via Sen George Murphy
from
Elvis Presley

FBI FILE PAGE WITH ANNOTATIONS IN ELVIS' HANDWRITING.

FEDERAL BUREAU OF INVESTIGATION

1

Date of transcription___**1/18/77**

—   D. BEECHER SMITH, II, was interviewed in the
presence of his law associate, FRANK J. GLANKLER, JR.,
and furnished the following information:

He is employed in the law firm of Montedonico,
Heiskell, Davis, Glankler, Brown and Gilliland, and maintains
his office at 1 Commerce Square, Memphis, Tennessee.

CHARLES H. DAVIS was a senior partner in this law
firm and had represented ELVIS A. PRESLEY and the PRESLEY
family interests for approximately 21 years. ELVIS PRESLEY
maintains a residence at Memphis, Tennessee, and is a
popular movie star and entertainer.

Due to the poor health of CHARLES DAVIS, D. BEECHER
SMITH became involved in the PRESLEY interests in behalf of
the law firm, and in this connection the following facts came
to his attention:

ELVIS PRESLEY owned a Lockheed Jetstar airplane,
registration number N777EP and manufacturer's serial number
5004.

In June, 1976, there was an outstanding indebtedness
on the aircraft in excess of $600,000. This was owed to the
American National Bank of Morristown, New Jersey. This
particular bank held the mortgage on the plane since it was
purchased, according to SMITH, in the general area of this
bank.

This aircraft was not being used by PRESLEY in his
entertainment business and therefore he was making payments
on an asset that was not generating any return on its capital.
In addition, attempts to sell the aircraft have resulted in
no success.

A meeting was scheduled for June 24, 1976, to
arrange a transaction wherein the plane could be refinanced,
funds would be provided for its upgrading, and the plane
could be leased out and generate a return on the investment
of approximately $1,000 per month.

Interviewed on___**1/17/77**___at **Memphis, Tennessee**___File # **Memphis 87-16994**

by___**SA** ▮▮▮▮▮▮▮▮▮▮▮▮ *b7C*___Date dictated___**1/18/77**

3

ME 87-16994
2

NIGEL WINFIELD is President of the Commercial
Air-Transport Sales, 5553 Northwest 36th Street, Miami,
Florida 33166. His telephone is 305-887-1591. WINFIELD
had had business dealings in the purchase of airplanes by
PRESLEY and therefore was known to him for his capabilities
in this field of endeavor. WINFIELD, according to SMITH,
introduced VERNON PRESLEY to FREDERICK P. PRO. PRO was
identified as the President of Air Cargo Enigma, Inc.,
5533 Northwest 36th Street, Miami, Florida 33166. He has
telephone number 305-592-5420. VERNON PRESLEY is the father
of ELVIS PRESLEY and, acting with Power of Attorney, assists
ELVIS PRESLEY in his business interests.

Present at the meeting on June 24, 1976, were the
following individuals:

HANS P. ACHTMANN,
President of W.W.P. Leasing Group,
Suite 450, 230 Park Avenue,
New York City
(212-689-9430);

NIGEL WINFIELD;

FREDERICK P. PRO;

GABRIEL ROBERT CAGGIANO, Attorney,
210 Commercial Street
Boston, Massachusetts
(subsequently determined to be a
corporate officer of
World Aircraft Exchange, Inc.,
1 Court Street, Boston, Massachusetts);

RAYMOND W. BARZNER,
Executive Vice President,
World Aircraft Exchange,
1 Court Street, Boston, Massachusetts;

LARRY WOLFSON, Treasurer,
Commercial Air-Transport Sales,
previously mentioned;

4

ME 87-16994
S

CHARLES H. DAVIS and D. BEECHER SMITH,
attorneys acting in behalf of ELVIS PRESLEY.

It is SMITH's recollection that WINFIELD, PRO and
CAGGIANO had promoted the idea of a sale-lease plan involving
sub-leasing of the Jetstar and including an upgrading of the
plane.

The transaction contemplated involved the sale of
the Jetstar by ELVIS PRESLEY (through his father, VERNON
PRESLEY acting under Power of Attorney) to W.W.P. Leasing
Group. W.W.P. was to borrow enough money from the Chemical
Bank of New York to cover both paying off of the present
indebtedness on the aircraft, which is over $600,000, and
also upgrading this aircraft in order to qualify it for
Federal Aviation Regulation 121 Maintenance Program. This
upgrading had an estimated cost of $350,000.

Upon completion of the upgrading, the plane allegedly
would be valued on the open market at approximately $950,000.
With W.W.P. purchasing the plane, the contractual agreement
was for ELVIS PRESLEY to lease the plane back for 84 months
(7 years) at a monthly rental of $16,755. Thereafter PRESLEY
would sub-lease the plane for $17,755 per month for 84 months
to Air Cargo Express. This would result in a $1,000 a month
profit for PRESLEY, and at the end of the 7-year period
PRESLEY had the right to buy back the plane for $1.00. However,
the contractual agreement would allow Air Cargo to continue
another three years, paying a reduced rental of $10,000 per
month.

BASZNER was present at this meeting because he,
acting as agent of World Aircraft Exchange, Inc., was supposed
to be responsible for supervising the upgrading and modification of the aircraft to qualify it for the Federal Aviation
Regulation (FAR) 121 Maintenance Program.

CAGGIANO claimed to be representing Air Cargo
Express (FRED PRO), according to SMITH, but later told SMITH
that he was representing World Aircraft Exchange (BASZNER).

The meeting of June 24, 1976, had to be delayed
over into June 25 for the actual signing of the contract.
HANS ACHTMANN had to leave on the evening of June 24 and
asked CAGGIANO to assist on the following day with the
completion of the lease agreement between W.W.P. and ELVIS
PRESLEY.

5

ME 87-16994
4

SMITH has no knowledge of any prior association between CAGGIANO and ACHTMANN but feels the request of CAGGIANO was made because of his familiarity with the entire transaction, as well as his abilities as an attorney.

WINFIELD and WOLFSON were present at this meeting because WINFIELD was the aircraft broker and WOLFSON works with him.

SMITH said that the purpose of the meeting on the 24th was not clear to him at its commencement because he had only been called upon by his law associate, CHARLES DAVIS, a few minutes prior to the commencement of the meeting. Due to some changes in the sub-lease agreement, the transaction which originally had been contemplated to be closed in May had been delayed one month.

ACHTMANN had given CAGGIANO a standard form lease consisting of one page, front and back, with approximately 30 short paragraphs and provisions covering the lease agreement for any particular chattel, which in this case was the airplane. CAGGIANO was to complete this lease agreement on June 25, 1976, and return the executed contract to ACHTMANN. The delay in the execution of the contract was due to Mr. DAVIS' poor health and it was to be resumed the following day.

It was on this following day, June 25, 1976, that SMITH learned BASZNER, on behalf of World Aircraft Exchange, would handle the supervising of the upgrading of the aircraft in order for it to qualify for the FAR 121 Maintenance.

Riders were drafted by Messrs. SMITH, DAVIS, and CAGGIANO, including life insurance, hull insurance, and liabilities.

There was also a provision that the purchase money would be released first to American National Bank to pay off the outstanding indebtedness, then certain funds would go to Air Cargo Express for upgrading the plane, and the balance of the funds were to be released to World Aircraft Exchange for supervising, directing and reporting on the upgrading of the aircraft as statements were issued for services rendered.

6

ME 87-16994
5

On June 25, 1976, the lease agreement was signed by VERNON PRESLEY, acting for ELVIS PRESLEY, and he paid two checks to W.W.P., both in the amount of $16,755, representing the first and 84th monthly rental payments. At the same time FRED PRO wrote three checks to ELVIS PRESLEY, two in the amount of $17,755 each, representing the first and 84th monthly payments, and the third representing a premium for the sub-lease, as required under the sub-lease agreement, in the amount of $40,000. CAGGIANO took his copies of the documents and left; PRO took the keys to the Jetstar and his copies of the documents and left; and PRESLEY took his checks from PRO along with his (PRESLEY's) copies of the documents and left.

However, shortly thereafter it was determined that none of the checks furnished by PRO to PRESLEY were valid and all were returned by the bank.

Later during a telephonic contact with PRO, SMITH was told that the money was coming from Jamaica or some place else and that there had been an error in the transfer of funds.

About a week later, SMITH learned that the Chemical Bank of New York, which was involved in the negotiation of the lease by PRESLEY from W.W.P., reported that the standard chattel lease agreement was unacceptable, and they provided their own draft of the agreement, consisting of approximately 23 pages, to embody the terms of the agreement between ELVIS PRESLEY and W.W.P.

On Tuesday, July 13, 1976, SIDNEY ZNEIMER, an attorney for W.W.P., came to Memphis with the document, and certain changes were made with the approval of ZNEIMER as spokesman for W.W.P. and the Chemical Bank of New York. While ZNEIMER was in the law office with SMITH and DAVIS, CAGGIANO and BASZNER arrived unannounced. BASZNER had certain invoices for payment for upgrading on the aircraft. DAVIS did not want VERNON PRESLEY to sign them as BASZNER desired, because under the original rider of the lease, the release of funds for upgrading was the responsibility of W.W.P. PRESLEY then, with the approval of the attorneys, signed these invoices evidencing approval that W.W.P. make the payments as it was not desired that PRESLEY be placed in a position of supervising the upgrading and modification of the airplane.

7

ME 87-16994 (
7   EXHIBIT E

WORLD AIRCRAFT EXCHANGE INC.

Executive Offices:
One Court Street
Boston, Mass. 02105
U.S.A.
227-3155

Statement 106 E.P.
July 7, 1976

W.W.P. Leasing Corp.
230 Park Avenue
New York, New York

Per Lease Amendment Document between W.W.P. Leasing Corp. and
Elvis A. Presley, this statement will serve to authorize a
disbursement of funds in the amount specified below to the
following party:

Amount: $17,500.00

Payee: Frederick P. Pro, President, Air Cargo Express Inc.

For: Certification for F.A.A. 121 per Agreement,
Operational Setup and Flight Management

Approved for payment by
W. W. P. Leasing Corp.

Elvis A. Presley

By: *[signature]*

Per Power of Attorney

THE PRESLEY CONNECTION: DOCUMENTS THAT CHRONICLE THE PRESLEY FAMILY'S ROLE
IN THE GOVERNMENT-SPONSORED STING OPERATION AGAINST THE ORGANIZED-CRIME
GROUP KNOWN AS THE FRATERNITY.

ME 87-16994
9   (

WORLD AIRCRAFT EXCHANGE INC.

Executive Offices:
O· · Court Street
B. ·· ·n, Mass. 0210S
U.S.A.
617 227-3155

Statement 306 E.P.
July 7, 1976

W.W.P. Leasing Corp.
230 Park Avenue
New York, New York

Per Lease Amendment Document between W.W.P. Leasing Corp. and
Elvis A. Presley, this statement authorizes the disbursement
of funds, in the amount specified below to the following party:

     Amount: $129,500.00

     Payee: Trans World Industries Inc.

     For: Part 121 Maintenance Systems,
                Certification and Modification,
                Cardex System

                            Approved for payment by
                            W. W. P. Leasing Corp.

                            Elvis A. Presley
                            By:
                            Per Power of Attorney

ME 87-16994
11
WORLD AIRCRAFT EXCHANGE INC.

Executive Offices:
One Court Street
Boston, Mass. 02103
U.S.A.
617 227-3155

Statement: 506 E.P.
July 7, 1976

W.W.P. Leasing Corp.
230 Park Avenue
New York, New York

Per Lease Amendment Document between W.W.P. Leasing Corp. and
Elvis A. Presley, this statement will authorize the disbursement
of funds, in the amount specified below, to the following
party:

Amount: $117,500.00

Payee: Frederick P. Pro, President, Air Cargo Express Inc.

For: Port 121 Inspection and Operational Flight Proving
      Tests and Aircraft Improvement Program, i.e. Pur-
      chase of Service Bulletin 230, A - E.

117,500
78,510
───────
38,990

Approved for payment by

W. W. P. Leasing Corp.

Elvis A. Presley

By:

Per Power of Attorney

13

24

ME 87-16994

DETAILS:

Investigation in this case was predicated upon
receipt of a request from Assistant United States Attorney
GLEN GARLAND REID, advising that he had been contacted
by attorneys D. BEECHER SMITH and JAMES N. RAINES of a
Memphis law firm who are representing the interests of
ELVIS A. PRESLEY. PRESLEY is described by them as a
television and motion picture star and entertainer. Mr.
REID had reviewed the account presented to him by the
attorneys and felt an investigation should be instituted
to determine if a violation of the Fraud By Wire Statute
did in fact exist.

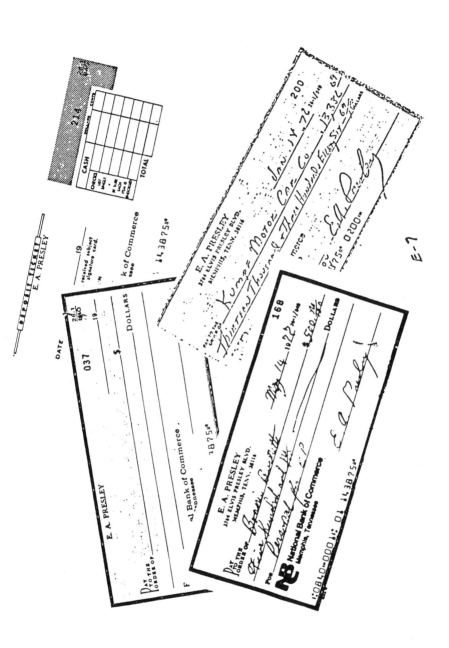

THE WHITE HOUSE	THE DAILY DIARY OF PRESIDENT JIMMY CARTER		

THE WHITE HOUSE
WASHINGTON, D.C.

DATE (Mo., Day, Yr.)
JUNE 14, 1977

TIME   DAY
? p.m. TUESDAY

TIME		PHONE	ACTIVITY
From	To	P = Placed / R = Rec'd	
?			The President and the First Lady met with: Otto Hinrichsen, President of the Partners of Amercias Organization, Recife, Brazil and former participant in the Brazil/Georgia exchange program when the President was Governor of Georgia Harry S. "Scott" Burnett, Staff Assistant
5:15			The President returned to his private office.
			The President met with:
5:15	5:30		Mr. Jordan
5:15	5:25		Mr. Moore
5:15	5:25		James C. Free, Associate for Congressional Liaison
5:15	5:30		Mr. Powell
5:18	5:24	P	The President talked with entertainer Elvis Presley.
5:27	5:~~	R	The President talked with Secretary Brown.
5:37	5	'	The President talked with the Rev. Mr. King.
5:43	5:	R	The President talked Secretary Califano.
5:53	6:01	R	The President talked with Administrator of the Drug Enforcement Administration, Peter B. Bensinger.
6:C8			The President returned to the second floor Residence.
6:08	6:09	R	The President talked with his Personal Assistant and Secretary, Susan S. Clough.
6:47		R	The President was telephoned by Orville R. Harris, professor emeritus, University of Virginia, Charlottsville, Virginia. Mrs. Yates took the call.
7:15			The President had dinner with: The First Lady Amy Carter Chip and Caron Carter
8:55			The President returned to his private office.
9:03		P	The President telephoned Clark M. Clifford, partner with Clifford, Warnke, Glass, McIllwain, and Finney law firm, Washington, D.C. and personal emissary of the President to Greece, Turkey and Cyprus. The call was not completed.

GPO : 1977 O – 228-197

Page 4 of 5 Page(s).

FROM PRESIDENT JIMMY CARTER'S WHITE HOUSE CALENDAR.

E Dr

THE WHITE HOUSE
WASHINGTON

TELEPHONE MEMORANDUM

President,   June 14, 19 77

TIME PLACED	DISC	NAME	ACTION
OUT / INC **AM** 743 PM	744	Sec. Califano. X 7437	ok. n.y.
INC OUT **AM** 7-55 PM	8-11	Mrs. Carter *n.y*	taping ok 8-09
INC OUT **AM** 8-04 PM	8-08	Secy Califano *ny*	ok
INC OUT **AM** 8-12 PM	8-13	Mrs. Carter	ok
INC OUT **AM** 12⁰⁰ᴺ PM	12⁰¹	X 6487 Achsah Nesmith	ok
INC OUT **AM** 12¹⁰ PM	12¹³	Burt Lance (mess)	ok 12¹²
INC OUT **AM** 1.05 PM	1.12	Cong Ed Jenkins *ny* 225-5211 w T House floor	on floor - les ok 1.10 p
INC OUT **AM** 4:57 PM	5.42	Rev. Martin Luther King *n.y.* 404-688-7300 Sr.	ok 5.37 P
INC OUT **AM** 5:18 PM	5:24	Elvis Presley 901-332-1777	ok
INC OUT **AM** 5:27 PM	5:30	Jeo. Brown	ok
INC OUT **AM** 543 PM	5.51	Secy Califano 225-5417	ok

(Speaker's *ofc*)

ELVIS DISPLAYS ONE OF HIS MANY LAW ENFORCEMENT BADGES.

CONTENTS OF THE PRESLEY FILE.

8

BEHIND CLOSED DOORS

O n January 8, 1986, when Tim Malloy, coanchor of a news segment on KCOP TV in Los Angeles, introduced the voice of KCOP's reporter Bob Walsh and then showed what is now known as the Poolhouse Picture, the world took notice. In the words of KCOP:

> Mike Joseph took his family to Graceland for a vacation on January 1st of 1978, more than four months after the death of Elvis Presley—perhaps we should say "reported death." At the time the grounds of Graceland were the only part of the estate open to the public, but Joseph took snapshots and put them away for safekeeping. Four years later while reading about Presley, Joseph took out his mementos of the Graceland visit, and he noticed something unusual in a shot of the bathhouse behind the mansion. It was a shadow in the lower half of the door. Joseph says he had the picture enlarged and the results were nothing short of startling. Someone or something bearing a remarkable resemblance to Elvis Presley was indeed sitting behind the door… The sequence of pictures including shots of Elvis's grave confirms that the pictures were indeed taken after Presley's death. Joseph says he's not trying to convince anyone that Elvis still lives or that the

snapshot is an image of some supernatural phenomenon but there is something there. How it got there and what it is will no doubt remain as much a mystery as the entire Presley mystique.

Two years later, in February 1988, on *Breakthrough*, an independent TV telemarketing program shown across the nation on a number of stations, Mr. Joseph was interviewed by Leonard Grant. During the course of the show, Mr. Joseph said:

One day, after reading a book, I decided to look at my pictures again. I pulled them out and this time I saw something in one of the pictures that I hadn't seen in over the years. Of course, I wasn't really studying them. But the sun had just hit on this picture in such a way that it picked up this image sitting in the doorway—a shadow in the doorway. For curiosity's sake, not that I would know who was there, I wanted to see what it was. I took my son's magnifying glass, put it on the picture, and started pulling it away from the picture to get a good visible view of it and I was just shocked. I couldn't believe what I saw. My God! I had Elvis Presley sitting in the doorway, looking out at the fans walking past his grave.

Why? I asked myself a million times. Why? I don't know. Did he fake his death? Did he have to fake his death? Why couldn't he go off to an island someplace? Lock himself up in Graceland. I mean, I understand he stayed inside his house for months at a time. I remember the night of the vigil. There were something like 80,000 people outside the gates of Graceland. All of a sudden a car with teenagers in it—they were intoxicated—ran into the crowd, hit three women, two died. Maybe he was gonna come back—come back for the ultimate comeback. He was a practical joker. Maybe now he can't come back because of this accident.

When Mr. Joseph was asked how we could be sure the photographs had not been tampered with, Joseph replied they were "the only negatives I've had" and that he'd had the negatives examined by Kodak: "They were taken in sequence, uncut. By the negatives being original they can tell. The emulsion number of the film was manufactured in '77. A roll of film has a manufacturing date in the emulsion number. You couldn't pay Kodak to say something like that if it weren't true." (There is a letter from Kodak testifying to this analysis.)

Interviewer Grant then wondered aloud how Joseph knew it was Elvis in the chair and not simply a photograph. Joseph replied: "Because we have a photograph here that shows the chair, empty, that he was sitting in. In photograph number four it shows I was taking the shot of the people with the background of the house, the bathhouse there. And we happened to close in on that and there's just an empty chair. It is said to have been one of Elvis's favorite chairs, one in which he sometimes got his hair cut."

Elaborating on the series of shots, Joseph explained: "We couldn't go near the house. This is a security guard's car. Things were sorta makeshift. It was too early; it [the mansion] wasn't opened up as a museum yet, so the house was closed to the public. Uh, this is Elvis's headstone, and right here in the corner is his mother's. So this shows that this was taken after August 16, 1977, and before '79, when his father died, because his father would be right over here, and in '80 his grandmother, Minnie Mae. This is the shot that I took of people walking and the bathhouse in the distance. We zero in here, and this is the same shot with just the chair, no one sitting in the chair. [Elvis] would be seeing us—and the people walking past his headstone."

Mr. Joseph gave other interviews, such as one to *The Globe* (January 18, 1983), basically detailing the same story. I, along with countless others, met with Mike Joseph, and he repeated the above observations.

After the Poolhouse Picture became known to Graceland, the original poolhouse door was replaced with a solid door. No one could see inside.

Mike Joseph's picture is still remarkable and shocking.

As an added note: Some have suggested that the man sitting behind the poolhouse door is Elvis lookalike Johnny Harra, who was cast in the docudrama *This Is Elvis*, filmed in part at Graceland. However, *This Is Elvis* was not filmed until more than two years later.

By the way, beside the pool itself was a plaque with Elvis's name on it with the birthdate 1935 followed by the date of death, which reads: "Never." This plaque was removed a few years ago.

Because a picture may indeed be worth a thousand words, those wishing further information on the Poolhouse Picture are invited to send a stamped, self-addressed envelope to: The Arctic Corporation, P.O. Box 6134, Gainesville, GA 30504.

A sequence of credibly documented Elvis sightings involves Kalamazoo, Michigan. Before Elvis's death—December 3, 1976— during Elvis's last Vegas engagement, Elvis was onstage joking with his audience. Responding to a girl in the front row about his living in Memphis, Elvis's reply was thus taped and transcribed:

> **Elvis:** Honey, I don't even live in Tennessee, that's all a
> joke. I live in—uh—no…
> **Audience:** L.A., Alabama, Honolulu, Hawaii?
> **Elvis:** Uh, no, I don't—no. That place in Michigan.
> **Audience:** Lansing? Pontiac? Detroit? Grand Rapids…?
> **Elvis:** No, not Lansing, not Pontiac, what's that place?
> Kalamazoo…

Adding yet more corroboration to Elvis and the Kalamazoo connection (and subsequent reported sightings) is that on August 17, 1977, the headlines of *The Kalamazoo Gazette* read: ELVIS SAW KALAMAZOO INCOGNITO. The story went on to state that Elvis saw the city from the window of a nondescript 1970 Buick sometime prior to his death and was very impressed with the city and of the treatment he received. No one knows exactly what Elvis was looking for, but it would be well to note that Elvis had performed in Kalamazoo previously and later at Wings Stadium.

Others in and around Kalamazoo have reported seeing a man by the name of Jon or John Burrows going into an old hotel that stood dormant for some time before being renovated into private offices. The management of that complex denies that either Mr. Burrows or Mr. Presley have anything to do with the complex. However, one radio interviewer, because of the increasing number of reported Elvis sightings in Kalamazoo, did call the complex and ask to speak to Mr. John/Jon Burrows. Messages for this man, who wasn't there, were taken. Eventually the radio interviewer was called back and told there was no Mr. John/Jon Burrows, then was asked, "But what did you want with Mr. Burrows, anyway?"

Recall that "Jon Burrows" is the pen name Elvis used in his letter to President Nixon.

Much of the public is aware that boxer Muhammad Ali and Elvis Presley were close friends. Beyond the fact that Muhammad Ali's farm is just outside Kalamazoo (Ali's outgoing mail is postmarked Kalamazoo), in a 1979 magazine interview with *Modern People*, Ali described Elvis: "…my close personal friend. Elvis came to my Deer Lake training camp about two years before he died. He told us he didn't want nobody to bother us. He wanted peace and quiet and I gave him a cabin in my camp and nobody even knew it. When the cameras started watching me train, he was up on the hill sleeping in the cabin. Elvis had a robe made for me [for one of Muhammad Ali's fights]. I don't admire nobody, but Elvis Presley was the sweetest, most humble and nicest man you'd want to know."

In a 1989 *Esquire* magazine piece entitled "Great Men Die Twice," interviewer Mark Kram reminded Ali of a statement made by him concerning Elvis: "Elvis, you have to keep singing or die to stay big…"

Another Kalamazoo-Elvis link involves entertainer Wayne Newton (who also, as recounted later in this book, had a connection to Operation Fountain Pen). At a March 18, 1990, live concert in Kalamazoo, Michigan, Newton addressed the audience, asking if any of them had seen him out walking that day. No one in the audience responded with a yes. Newton repeated the question and received the same response. He then asked: "Do you mean no one saw me out walking today? See, that's how Elvis does it. In fact, Elvis was with me. He loves this brisk weather."

Perhaps this remark was said in jest. But what about the reply Newton made on Nashville's *Crook and Chase* television show on January 8, 1991, in response to a question posed to him about Elvis? Mr. Newton's reply: "There is no doubt in my mind that his [Elvis's] soul is not fulfilled yet," Newton said quietly and seriously. "And we will be seeing him again, too."

By and far the most intriguing and in-depth Kalamazoo sighting involves Kelly Burgess, a former assistant editor and feature writer with the *Detroit News*. Like much of the world, Kelly was skeptical about the many rumors of Elvis sightings in Michigan, Kalamazoo in particular. Nevertheless, she decided to drive there from Detroit to investigate.

Here for the first time is a transcript of the taped interview she gave on *The Billy Goodman Show* in the fall of 1988, broadcast via KBEG Radio, Las Vegas—commercials omitted (Kelly also gave a TV interview to Mr. Goodman):

BILLY GOODMAN KBEG RADIO
INTERVIEW WITH KELLY BURGESS

ELVIS-KALAMAZOO CONNECTION
INVESTIGATION OF A REPORTED ELVIS PRESENCE

BG: We will be listening to Kelly Burgess. Kelly actually met Elvis Presley in August of this year, and she's going to tell us what happened at that meeting. Welcome back to this "story behind the story" in the Elvis Presley controversy—whether he's dead or alive. Our next guest is Kelly Burgess.

Kelly, you've got quite a background, *Detroit News*—tell us something about yourself.

KB: Well, for ten years I was an editorial feature writer and sometime columnist on the staff of the *Detroit News*.

BG: ...and there came a time when you left the *Detroit News*?

KB: Yes, I left the *Detroit News*—since then I've been writing for national magazines. I have an article in this month's issue of *Skin*

Diver magazine.

BG: I understand that you actually talked to Elvis. This is great. Tell us about it. How did you ever even think of trying to find him—where did you find him? Let's start from how you got there. Take us on your trip that you told us about today—it's interesting.

KB: First of all, unfortunately, I was never an Elvis fan. I never had the opportunity to see a concert, never owned a record. When he died, I felt very bad, but it just kind of passed, and I never gave it a second thought until this summer. I don't know if any of you had access to the Michigan newspapers. There were several sightings of him in Michigan, and that's where I'm from—Troy, Michigan, which is a suburb of Detroit. About the same time, I read Gail Giorgio's book *Is Elvis Alive?* and I became quite intrigued by the research that she did, and what she had uncovered. And the more I read about the sightings in Kalamazoo—as a reporter—it was a challenge. One day, around the first week in August, I told my twenty-two-year-old son, "Let's go to Kalamazoo today." I went totally expecting to find nothing. I had heard about the lookalike. And when we arrived in Kalamazoo, we went to the Burger King, and to the YMCA.

BG: Tell everybody what happened at the YMCA. We can't let that get by.

KB: I went to the YMCA and spoke to the director of the fitness center and I said, "Does Elvis Presley work out here?" He said, "Just a minute, I'll have to check the roster."

BG: I think that's great, I really do. Nonchalant as can be...

KB: ...which he did, and he came back and said, "No. Elvis Presley does not work out here." Let me tell you first that there is a lookalike running around Kalamazoo creating an uproar. Many people have seen him; he hangs around the Burger King, goes into the super-market, could be spotted driving a car. I've even heard he throws parties and invites people and hands out T-shirts. That is not Elvis Presley.

BG: Where did you find Elvis Presley?

KB: I went to an old hotel on Main Street. Now, Kalamazoo is a small college town with very antiquated buildings. I went to this hotel, which was built in the 1890s—there's a renovation underway there now—it's being converted from an old hotel into an office complex. Three gentleman bought the hotel in 1985.

BG: Where did you find Elvis?

KB: You want to hear the details? The mystery behind it?

BG: Well, maybe we could go back afterwards to it. Where did you find Elvis is what I want to know.

KB: I went into the building and started surveying. [**AUTHOR'S NOTE:** I believe Kelly's son remained outside.] There's five stories, a five-story building with an atrium elevator. I started surveying every floor. I had three encounters with security guards. I was not intimidated by the guards. They told me to leave. They said, "You're not allowed in here." My next step was to go into some of the offices; there are several tenants doing business in that building. I went into offices asking for Elvis Presley or John Burrows. They all looked at me, quite incredible. I mean, here's these business people and I'm asking for Elvis Presley. At one point some of the people said, "Elvis is not here, but we've seen his illegitimate son, Elvis Presley, Jr.," which turned out to be a joke. The last office I went into was off the main floor and lobby. I spoke to the receptionist and asked the same question. She said, "Just a moment, I'll get my manager." So the manager came out and I was speaking to him about Elvis, and he seemed quite interested, and asked my reason for being here. We talked about five minutes; I had my back to the office door. Suddenly he said, "There's the man you want to see," and I turned around. Elvis was standing there; it was almost as if lightning had struck in that room!

BG: You're there—it was Elvis. Tell us about what happened then.

KB: His presence was overwhelming. Now mind you, I've been a reporter; I've seen and worked on all kinds of stories. This was the first time in my life that I was stunned. I didn't know what to say. He took his finger—like this—and said, "What are you doing in this building bothering the tenants? I will not have this." He was very angry. I said, "I'm with the *Detroit News* and I'm doing a story on Elvis."

"I do not care if you're with the *Detroit Star*, I will not have this!"

Yet in the next moment his mood changed entirely. He was very kind. I could feel that he did not feel threatened by me; I was not aggressive. I started talking to him and he did not say a word for about five minutes. I started outlining some of the facts in Giorgio's book: "Why didn't anyone collect life insurance? And why didn't Vernon accept the flag for the coffin?" He stood there and listened; he didn't say one word. At one point I turned around and he was standing at a kind of angle. I turned so that I could look directly into his eyes. He had on gold-rimmed glasses, a modified version of what he used to wear; they had a slight tint to them. But I looked in his eyes, and he had the Elvis Presley expression in his eyes, which I think that most people that knew him are familiar with—that kind of sparkle—the same-shaped eyes, same-color eyes. Again, I was stunned. It was shining through, what comes through all of us that says, "This is me." It's kind of your soul that shines through your eyes. I said, "You have eyes just like Elvis. Are you a relative?" He said, "Nope."

See, for some reason, and today I still don't know why, I did not let him know that I thought he was Elvis. I still don't know why. I didn't come out and ask him. After he listened to my questions, he just stood there with a very pleasant look on his face, smiling at times. Just before I walked away, he said, "Yeah, but it's against the law to hoax your death." And I left the building, but then I returned. Should I talk about that?

BG: What did you return for?"

KB: To take a picture, to…

BG: Kelly, what does Elvis Presley look like?

KB: He's about six feet, maybe 195 pounds, with a small pot-belly. He looked really good. He had a head of very thick white hair, without sideburns; his hair was done up in a kind of boyish haircut. Same mouth, same high cheekbones. I mean, it was Elvis. Anyway, I followed him into the construction office and he sat down at his desk. Then he put his head down. He spoke very little in the short time that I saw him. I thought he was looking for a pen so he could write my number down. Evidently he didn't find one and I didn't. I ripped out a deposit slip from my checkbook and handed it to him.

He said, "All right, Kelly." And I left. After that I did get several hang-ups and hold-ons on my answering machine. It was quite an experience. I'll never forget it for the rest of my life.

BG: I wouldn't think you would.

KB: I mean, his presence was just electrifying.

BG: You, like everyone else, knew it was him—the vibrations and everything that goes with it, that it was Elvis. Kelly, I understand that you're writing a book?

KB: Yes, I am.

BG: What's it going to be about?

KB: It's going to be about Elvis Presley, from 1977 to 1988.

BG: You're going to tell what he's been doing. How about giving us some inside information?

KB: No. I'm sorry. I can't do that."

Kelly Burgess was a credible lady. She was not the new kid on the block careerwise, but a mature woman with grown children. (When I was invited to appear on *Geraldo*, Kelly agreed to appear with me; but, like all other credible guests I was promised, Kelly was "uninvited" prior to the show on the grounds that she was "too credible.")

In a later telephone call with Kelly, she related that she had uncovered evidence that was frightening and shocking. When I asked her if she had gotten a picture of Elvis that day, she said she'd rather not say. After that Kelly told me that she was dropping the idea of the book because the evidence she had uncovered was dangerous and she felt that a noninvolved posture was best.

"Does it have anything to do with the mob?" I asked.

"Yes," she replied hesitantly. "It does…"

***

Is everyone who is otherwise credible simply making it all up when it comes to Elvis? Even Harold Schuitmaker, a well-known Michigan politician and resident of Paw Paw (15 miles outside of Kalamazoo) said, "Elvis is alive and living in Kalamazoo. That is what I understand. I have not seen him personally, but I know people who have and I trust those people. Why Kalamazoo? It's a good place to hide." (*Detroit News*, August 22, 1988.)

And last but not least, Elvis himself said it while on stage less than a year before what was widely reported as his death.

9

MYSTERY CALLER

In October of 1988, a few months after the date Kelly Burgess said she met with Elvis, I received a telephone call from a man who identified himself as Elvis Presley. This call came in the wee hours of the morning, but luckily I was functioning well enough to be able to tape the call.

Knowing, of course, there are hundreds of Elvis impersonators, I asked key questions regarding a close friend we had in common, Mae Axton. Mae not only introduced Elvis to the Colonel but is best known for having cowritten Elvis's first million seller, the song "Heartbreak Hotel." Since I had also known Mae since the mid-1950s, I knew the story behind the story: exactly how, when, and where this song was born. I felt it unlikely that an impersonator would know the intricacies of the hows, whens, and wheres of the creation of the song "Heartbreak Hotel."

Not only did the "Voice-on-the-Telephone" know the correct story, he was able to elaborate upon it. Later, when I checked these elaborations out with Mae, she was startled. "Yes! That part's true. I had forgotten all about that!" I played her the taped call and again she was shocked. "That sounds just like Elvis—it has to be Elvis…"

Mae spoke about the familiar nuances in his voice, the way he used phrases, the tone and depth, and since she probably knew Elvis's voice as well as anyone's voice, I felt confident that the possibility of the caller's being Elvis was higher than usual.

Some of the topics and incidents discussed with the man who identified himself as Elvis:

· He was in a state of shock over Lisa Marie's marriage (to Danny Keough).
· He was at the wedding, as was Priscilla.
· He told me not to ask him about people in particular because he did not want to get others involved.
· He used the term "Ricky" versus my term "Rick" (referring to Rick Stanley).
· When asked how the world will accept Elvis Presley as being a grandfather, he said, "It's how I'll accept it…"
· Wax dummy in coffin.
· Health problems.
· Weight problems.
· Drug stories.
· Disappointments.
· Press.
· Kindness and cruelties.

The following transcript is taken from the tape. This is the first time its contents have been published:

(If you wish information about ordering a copy of the taped "Voice," please send a stamped, self-addressed envelope to: The Arctic Corporation, P.O. Box 6134, Gainesville, GA 30504. Although the taped voice is not professionally clear—because the telephone call was neither planned nor expected—it's easier to follow along with the transcript. It's wonderful to listen to, and endearing.)

TRANSCRIPT OF TAPED TELEPHONE CALL

From: A man who identified himself as **Elvis Presley (EP)**.
To: Journalist/author **Gail Giorgio (GG)**.
Date: October 10, 1988 (tape available).

[**AUTHOR'S NOTE:** Since I only had an old-fashioned tape recorder, one with a suction cup, the first part of the tape is weak, while I held down the suction cup, the second half is easier to hear.]

October 1988 telephone call
Side 1 of tape:

EP: I understand they're giving you a rough time.

GG: Yeah'll. It's been strange, I'll say that…

EP: [inaudible] You don't have to worry.

GG: Where are you calling from?

EP: I can't say…[inaudible]

GG: What has happened?

EP: I'm dissatisfied with certain things…[inaudible]

GG: Is this Elvis Presley?

EP: Ah, yeah'll [inaudible] but I can't say about the official person, [inaudible]. It's been crazy…[inaudible]

GG: Have you talked to Mae Axton?

EP: [inaudible]…she's been [inaudible] about my music; it's been a lifetime ago since we touched bases…

GG: Has she known about this?

EP: One thing I have to be clear [inaudible]. I can't [inaudible] say certain things about people until something happens. [inaudible]…they'll go after other people. [inaudible] It's a weird situation.

GG: Have you done albums?

EP: I sing, but I, ah, never do an album per se [inaudible]. Most of the time I'm not serious at all. [laugh] I, ah, ah keep up with singing, but there's no pressure. I'm not serious about it. I'd have to sing in a different voice [inaudible]. Certain things [inaudible]…I've been doing so many different things. [inaudible] I've changed. [inaudible] People see me a certain way and I'm not that way anymore. I'm a different person. [inaudible]…new experiences and everything. [inaudible] Over a few years I've changed [inaudible]. It's crazy. [inaudible]

GG: What about Lisa Marie?

EP: Well, ah, that's the biggest thing in my life right now. The big

question is whether I'm in the way [inaudible]…wedding.
GG: You were at the wedding?
EP: [inaudible]
GG: Where was the wedding?
EP: It was at a church…[inaudible] Scientology [inaudible].
GG: What is Scientology about?
EP: It's ah, something [inaudible]…we disagree; I mean I was brought up with a different type of values and I [inaudible] that age…
GG: How old is Lisa?
EP: How old is she? She's twenty years old now [inaudible].
GG: I guess that's not too young to get married.
EP: I, I feel it is. I mean, it's not that I am able to voice my opinion as much as I'd like to. She's [inaudible] shock to me. [inaudible] She didn't mention a thing about it. I just pray now that she's happy…happy [inaudible]. I guess when you're twenty years old nowadays [inaudible]…[laughs slightly].
GG: Yeah'll…
EP: I mean I just hope she's [inaudible].
GG: Who did she marry?
EP: Ah, she married a guy she was going out with for quite some time. [inaudible] I can't complain, because he's a struggling young musician. [inaudible] I never met the guy until [inaudible]…marriage. [inaudible] I hope he treats her kind and everything.
GG: What's his name?
EP: The story hasn't come over from L.A., has it?
GG: No, ah…who did she marry?
EP: You haven't heard the story?
GG: I just heard she got married. I didn't know who she married.
EP: He's a young guy. She's known him for some years. I mean, ah, he plays in several different clubs around L.A. and everything…
GG: What is his name?
EP: He, ah, seems like a good guy, I mean, I can't complain because when I was his age I was very different. Like I say, he's ah, a little above the world [inaudible] to marry anyway. Like I said, she's twenty years of age, and ah, she felt it was right.
GG: When will she be twenty-one?

EP: In February.

GG: She's almost the same age as my daughter.

EP: She turns twenty-one February first.

GG: My daughter's birthday is February second.

EP: [inaudible]…so many different changes…

GG: What have you been doing?

EP: In the past year, the past ten years, or what [laugh]?

GG: [laugh]

EP: I mean there's so much [inaudible] to my life that people don't know about.

GG: Have you remarried?

EP: No.

GG: You've not remarried?

EP: I'm not saying [inaudible] now…[inaudible]

GG: Have you lost weight?

EP: I have, I ah, gained it back again, but I'm more at peace than when I was thin [inaudible]…mostly I've been working my voice and everything. [inaudible] diet. [inaudible] I talk to a lot of people…you'd be surprised. Actually, I tried to call you several times…

GG: I, ah, my phone rang or what?

EP: I figured with the circumstances [inaudible]…

GG: Why did you want to call me?

EP: There were sometimes that I thought you were wrong about different things you were saying…

GG: Probably quite a bit [laugh]. What was I wrong about?

EP: Ah, I can't name any specifics now, because, ah, as you say I'm [inaudible].

GG: Well, a lot of questions have been about the name spelled on the grave…?

EP: Well, that's something you're wrong about…

GG: Why?

EP: Well, it's something [inaudible] right about but not the reason why. There's a big story behind it, but…

GG: Well, I had always heard that your middle name was [pronounces the letters] A-R-O-N?

EP: Well, ah, originally that was right [inaudible]...long story.
GG: What was in the coffin?
EP: It wasn't me.
GG: Did you ever read the novel *Orion*?
EP: I heard different things about it, but I didn't read it...
GG: You didn't read it?
EP: [inaudible] I'm sorry, I didn't...
GG: I think you should read it. Is there any way I can get it to you?
EP: There's absolutely no way...especially right now. Maybe in the future.
GG: Well, ah, if you want it, I think you should read it.
EP: I've heard about it, but I never read it...
GG: Well, it will be back out in January, but you can order it...if I can't send it to you. But it's definite that you should read it.
EP: [inaudible]
GG: You don't write letters or anything?
EP: I never sign my name or anything. There's not really a need. My wants and everything are [inaudible].
GG: What about...I had received a letter from a man who was suffering from cerebral palsy; he had received letters from you prior to your leaving, and has since received birthday cards, letters...?
EP: [inaudible] but you've got to remember that for the last eleven years [inaudible]...
GG: But the fellow who owns the museum...?
EP: [inaudible]
GG: Did he know it was you?
EP: As far as I know. I talk to different people, and I've given certain things...if you want to check them out you can check them out, but I don't want to hurt [inaudible]. There's no one else I don't believe would know...
GG: Well, there's a lot of books written...
EP: I can't read every book, but I can believe that they...
GG: [laugh] Believe me, people know so much, I just heard...
EP: There's so many books, I mean, ah, I always said to the guys that there are people out here who know more about me than I do.
GG: I think so...

EP: It's just like you. You're asked certain questions and you probably can answer it.

GG: Well, I heard the drapes were made at Sears…?

EP: You're correct about that…

GG: [laugh] But I don't know where my drapes were made. Ah, what about Jimmy Gambill?

EP: What about him?

GG: Does he know?

EP: I can't—as I said earlier—I can't [inaudible] other people. I don't mean to be solemn or serious [laugh]. I can't talk about people, because then there'll be a lot of pressure on them, and that's not right. You know what I'm saying. [inaudible] But there's just certain people I can't [inaudible] say certain things. [inaudible]

GG: Well, how old is Jimmy now?

EP: Well, my head guy is named Jimmy now. But like I said, I can't answer any questions or tell you that I acknowledge anything. But I understand what you're saying; I respect that as a journalist. But I can't, ah…I can't answer certain questions. I might be able to, but [inaudible] right now [inaudible].

GG: How do you think all of this is going to end?

EP: I know it's going to end; I just don't know about the end result, or what everyone's reaction will be [inaudible].

GG: I think the reaction of people will be very positive.

EP: Well, I mean everybody is considerate of me, that type of thing, you know. People are very different now. You never know what's going to happen. That's my main concern, the people. I mean, I've been criticized and [inaudible] friends and relatives, and everything. I, I just don't know what the reaction will be. It worries me; it's my biggest fear…

GG: Well, I think the reaction will be very, very positive. I think people's reaction will be disbelief.

EP: That's what concerns me—I'll try to come back out, but people, you won't believe, that I've seen, people don't want to believe [inaudible] myself, but [inaudible] and everything…

[Here I asked the caller about some reported sightings of Elvis Presley.]

EP: Most of the people that have seen me don't know it's been me, but people that know for sure it's me [inaudible]. The whole thing comes down to, if people, if I came out, you, people expect what I look like. They'd, you know, probably [inaudible] go on, because people would think they're crazy, and that's what I've been banking on. People have seen me and looked me straight in the eye and [inaudible].

GG: Do you ever see Felton Jarvis?

EP: I told you about questions about people.

GG: Well, I just wondered if you see people like that?

EP: I've seen certain people [inaudible]. Yeah, I've talked to people, I've seen all the people [inaudible]. It's crazy. To me, it's [inaudible] exciting.

GG: Well, I think Felton made a statement, maybe he had seen you...so I just wondered...

EP: Well, I can't say anything [inaudible]...it's crazy. People are very surprised. [inaudible] I keep up with the latest news [inaudible]. I keep abreast of everything. I, I've been to so many different places people would never believe [inaudible]. This was before all these things happened, when you discovered certain things. You're just doing your thing...

GG: Well, if they didn't know you before, they wouldn't know you now, because they're looking for someone who looks more like you than you look like you.

EP: But I change me every day...

GG: Yeah'll...

EP: [inaudible] change my hair...

GG: Do you know a man named Sonny Neal?

EP: You're talking people again.

GG: Well, ah...sometimes I've gotten calls on radio stations from people sounding like Elvis Presley.

EP: They probably sound better than I do...I sing almost every night. [inaudible]

[Here I asked if he had heard the singer Orion sing; he said no.]

GG: Well now, how do I know who I'm talking to?

EP: There's no way of telling.

GG: What would be the point, I mean, of us talking?

EP: I mean, it's the same thing. I can only do the best I can. I will say if you [inaudible] I'm not the same person. I've done things to change me. I'll never be the same. There's no way I'll ever be the same.

GG: Well, let's see. Is there any question I can ask you?

EP: It's not the easiest [inaudible]. Other people have asked questions. There's no way I can answer them. Do you know who George is?

GG: George? No…

EP: He's a [inaudible]. He's the only one who would call when I was at Graceland, the only one [inaudible] it was an alias type of thing and the girls would get it [inaudible…(It sounded like he said "Queenie")] and they would run him right through. [inaudible]. You've got to understand the type of situation I'm in…

GG: Yeah'll. Well, ah, let's see…

EP: [inaudible]

GG: Who co-wrote "Heartbreak Hotel"? [The song "Heartbreak Hotel" is one of Elvis's biggest-selling early records.]

EP: It wasn't me. That's no secret. [inaudible] That was my first big break as far as…before that time I was [inaudible] just signed a big contract with [inaudible]…in my life [inaudible] she met me and she played it for me, anyway I was lucky, very lucky. I was not really known before I signed with RCA, I mean, ah, they took a big chance on me [inaudible]. She was a beautiful woman, she still is. That was centuries ago…

GG: Well, ah, there was another writer on "Heartbreak Hotel." [Besides Mae Axton.]

EP: The only thing I know, the recollection of the whole thing, there was this guy, I can't remember his name…she played the thing and I was crazy over it, and you know [inaudible] it was a different experience. I was very nervous. But I remember…I was a kid but I, I just tried to do my best. And that was it. No big deal. I was lucky that someone came up with that type of material. I, I was basically lucky…

GG: Where did you first hear "Heartbreak Hotel"?

EP: It was in a hotel room, it was in Memphis. I know it don't exist today, because, but I know it was a hotel room. She played it and I just remember, I can't remember specifically what I was doing or anything, but I just remember the tune and I went crazy for it, and I thought it was the type of song I could do and...

GG: Well, ah, when she played it, somebody else had already cut it or what?

EP: I'm not sure I understand...?

GG: Well, if she played the song, was it already on a tape, a piano or something...?

EP: She had a tape. Someone did it.

GG: Oh, okay. You weren't the first to cut it?

EP: No, you see the thing in the record business is one of two things, when they want to play you a song they wrote. They either sit down at a piano and play it...

GG: And then just tape it and play it for the artist?

EP: Or, or they do something else. They also bring a recording of it. Sometimes somebody's not established, they just sing the notes, the rhythm. They'll play it, you can see [inaudible] they have a certain guy that sings it, and in some cases it's a woman; they play it and you can hear it and...

GG: Did a woman first do "Heartbreak Hotel"?

EP: Oh, I can't remember what happened. It's one of two things that will happen. They'll sit down and they'll play it, or have a tape of someone doing it. It's fifty-fifty really. But I would say most of the time, most records I've heard, you know, unknown people do it— but most of the time it's unknown people and they give you a recording of the thing, and if I decide if I would like to [inaudible]. It's mostly a recording of someone singing, and sometimes people just sit down at a piano and do it themselves. It all depends on the situation. Sometimes it's a recording. A lot of times it's the writer or writers of a particular song—they'll sing it—and play a piano to it [inaudible]. It basically works the same way today —the writer will write a song, play it on the piano, sing it, [inaudible]. That's basically how it works [laugh]. Hasn't changed that much.

GG: Well, what are your plans now?

EP: To get over the shock of what I just went through—that's the main thing…

GG: Well, what will your future hold?

EP: God only knows, honey. I [laugh] I, I don't know myself. I think things are going to happen shortly, but I, well, you never know.

GG: Did you give Lisa away at the wedding?

EP: I, I wasn't able to…

GG: How come?

EP: It just wasn't possible. But I was there, I mean, I was [inaudible]. Everything was kept under wraps until it was done.

GG: When did she get married?

EP: [inaudible]

GG: I mean, was it recently?

EP: Very recently.

GG: I heard—somebody just told me something about it today.

EP: Very recent to me. I'm just the father [inaudible].

GG: When did your father—when did Vernon die?

EP: I can't talk about that at all.

GG: He did die, right?

EP: I can't comment on that one way or the other [inaudible].

GG: What about Dee Presley?

EP: What about her?

GG: She made a statement that she received a call from someone that sounded like Elvis saying things that only Elvis would have known.

EP: I could have at the time. I don't mean to sound like a politician [inaudible] but I've called many people [inaudible]. I call people all the time. Some hung up on me.

GG: Why? Oh, they didn't…?

EP: …believe me. But I expected it. It wasn't something I didn't expect. I, I expected that to happen. [inaudible] it hurt sometimes, but I mean, I expected it. But as far as calling people, I expect every time I call someone [inaudible]. I don't blame them, you know? I, I'd probably do the same thing.

GG: Well, are you still studying religion?

EP: I, I don't have to study it. It's more of a relaxing thing.

GG: Relaxing?

EP: [inaudible]...some things that bother me. As for the Bible, the Lord has got me through everything [inaudible].

GG: So your faith is still very deep?

EP: Oh, there's no way, no possible way—none of that will change. Obviously there's no way I could go through what I went...

[AUTHOR'S NOTE: At this point, the first side (side 1) of the tape ended. The other side (side 2) seemed to record more clearly, or I may have repositioned the suction cup better. Being the wee hours of the morning, now probably around 3:30 AM, my mind, not only having been in slumber, was constantly seesawing back and forth: Was it Elvis? Was this really Elvis I was speaking to? Was I being put on? Yet the episode having to do with Mae Axton and "Heartbreak Hotel" was true; Mae had played the tape for Elvis in an old hotel— one no longer there, the Andrew Jackson Hotel. It's not totally impossible an impersonator would know this information, but it's highly improbable.

Side 2 of the tape recording is somewhat clearer in most parts, and that is the part I agreed to have recopied on duplicates of the tape made for distribution.

This was also that side I brought with me to California, where I played it for Gene Smith, Elvis's first cousin (their mothers being sisters). Gene said it was definitely Elvis on the tape. It was as if he knew Elvis had indeed phoned.]

October 1988 telephone call
Side 2 of tape:

EP: I, I don't know. I just have to feel [out] other people, call and see...

GG: Ah, huh...

EP: I just have to [inaudible] and see [inaudible]. I do have to get going, ma'am. It's been very nice talking to you. I'm going to be leaving again, and so...

GG: Well, what do you want me to do from here on?

EP: There's not a heck of a lot you can do, really—it's up to me. Ya know...?

GG: Ah huh…

EP: [inaudible] around the world, my friends and family [inaudible]. It's up to me. There's nothing anybody else can really do. It's up to me to take charge of that type of a situation; it's just not up to them.

GG: Well, I certainly think it would help you to read the book *Orion*.

EP: Well [inaudible] recommended it or…

GG: No, the novel *Orion*. I think you should read it.

EP: I, I don't know. Well, anyway it's very nice talking with you. [inaudible] I just hope that everything goes—things will be happening very shortly.

GG: Well, ah, if they do and if the situation…

EP: I, I pray to God they do.

GG: Yeah'll…

EP: I don't want to be disappointed again.

GG: And if I can help you, will you let me?

EP: Oh, there's enough people involved now [laugh] as it is.

GG: Well, at least I have some direct connections with the press.

EP: I, I got enough of that.

GG: You don't think you need my help [laugh]? I can always call Larry King, right?

EP: But I mean, you know, certain things are happening—I can go somewhere now and you won't believe, so [inaudible]…

GG: Do you—when I was on the show with—I wasn't on actually— Sally Jessy Raphael Show, Rick Stanley was on. Do any of the Stanley boys know? [Rick Stanley—"Ricky" according to the caller—is one of Elvis's stepbrothers.]

EP: Again, I can't comment on that.

GG: I just wondered if they knew.

EP: I'll just say Ricky does not know. No matter about anybody else, obviously he does not know.

GG: Yeah'll…

EP: Ricky does not know.

GG: Do you think he's sincere in his religion?

EP: Oh, he's very sincere. There's no question. He's very religious. He still is. He always will be. I would never question that all. He's very sincere. We prayed countless times. So I know he's very sincere.

GG: Yeah'll. I know he went through a hard time. I guess according to…

EP: He went through his hard times. No question.

GG: Yeah'll…

EP: With drugs and alcohol and everything. He's found peace now, Jesus Christ, himself—he's got a family and everything.

GG: Do you still help a lot of people?

EP: I try to, but it's sometimes more difficult. Anyway, I, I don't mean to be rude but I do have to get going. Certain things are happening…

GG: Okay.

EP: [inaudible]

GG: Is there anybody that I can get in touch with if I needed to talk to you?

EP: Not really, ma'am. No, not really.

GG: Okay…

EP: I can't pass on that information. I'll try to touch bases with you. You tell me certain shows you're going to be on, I'll try to call you back.

GG: [laugh]

EP: I just never know…

GG: Well, let's see, ah…

EP: I just never know because—I watch every show but I just—with different time zones and things…

GG: Yeah'll. You're in a different time zone right now?

EP: Yes, ma'am.

GG: Okay. Well, ah, I will be moving; I may not have this number anymore. If you need to get hold of me, do you want another number?

EP: I don't see where it could hurt anything.

GG: Okay.

EP: I'm not saying—things are crazy but ah, if I can, I'll try.

GG: Okay. You can probably get ahold of me at [a certain telephone number that is no longer valid], if that doesn't change. I have to change my number often too.

EP: What area code would that be? [**AUTHOR'S NOTE:** Keep in mind the call was made to me by a man who described himself as a brother of someone who worked for Elvis, thus Elvis(?) did not actually dial the call.]

GG: It's 404.

EP: Well, ma'am, we'll see what happens. I guess you're a pretty busy woman yourself?

GG: Well, pretty busy writing books. I have—ah, *Orion* will be re-released in January, and I think it's a book that you should read. Then I have another book coming out in the spring. People have asked me to do a follow-up on the fans' reaction to the possibility of Elvis Presley being alive.

EP: That's crazy, man—he's dead!

GG: [laugh] Is he?

EP: If you saw me right now, you would say so.

GG: When does he become "alive" again?

EP: In a few hours. [laugh]

GG: Then he becomes "alive" again?

EP: I'm just waking up.

GG: Oh, you're just waking up…?

EP: Ah, I don't know, ah—it takes me a while, you see. I just had some major [inaudible] of my own.

GG: Major surgery?

EP: Major shock.

GG: What happened?

EP: Not surgery, major shock.

GG: What happened?

EP: My daughter and everything. It came as a surprise to me.

GG: Oh, okay…

EP: A very big surprise…

GG: Was Priscilla there?

EP: Priscilla's everywhere, if you read the newspapers…

GG: Well, I mean was she at the wedding?

EP: Yeah—she was there.

GG: Is she happy about it?

EP: You can ask her. Obviously [inaudible] but, she has her own people and everything…

GG: Well, maybe you'll be a grandfather one of these days? [At this time the news of Lisa's pregnancy had not been made public.]

EP: I'll definitely be out before I'm a grandfather.

GG: You'll definitely be out?

EP: The dust'll settle and everything. Believe me…

GG: How is the world going to react to Elvis Presley being a grand-father?

EP: It's not the question. It's how I'll react.

GG: [laugh] People have asked if it's a wax dummy in the coffin, and I laughingly say there was a wick at the top of the head.

EP: Well, thank goodness nobody, nobody lit it.

GG: [laugh] The great meltdown, huh?

EP: Worse than that. A, a nuclear reactor meltdown; the biggest story of a meltdown in history, ah…

GG: [laugh] Yeah'll, right.

EP: Well, I mean, you done a good job, and I just wanted to, ah, phone and—you're doing a good job and everything…

GG: Well, at least I'm defending the drug stories. I was on with Geraldo Rivera and yelled at him…

EP: If I was on as many drugs as they say I was, I guarantee you, I won't be talking.

GG: Do you have any medical problems yet?

EP: Oh, I got tons of 'em. [inaudible] but nothing serious. It's just a little nagging type of thing, but nothing that's life threatening. Except the marriage of my daughter.

GG: Yeah'll—is she on a honeymoon now?

EP: I can't comment on that. I can't say anything. Obviously she didn't go back to the house.

GG: Yeah'll…

EP: Well, it's been very nice talking with you, ma'am, and I wish you the best of luck, and ah…

GG: Well, thank you. I hope you'll call me again. And if you will, I'll send you a copy of *Orion*. You deserve to read it.

EP: I don't know what show you're going to be on, but hopefully I'll catch you.

GG: Okay. I'm sort of running out of shows. Right now I'm running out of steam. As I've said to people, you know, I might be able to find Elvis Presley, but I can't find my car keys. [laugh] Maybe something's wrong with this picture.

EP: I'll tell you what. I'll call you back sometime.

GG: Okay.

EP: Very soon…

GG: Thank you.

EP: And I'll tell you something: I don't mind people making money; that's the American dream.

GG: That's right.

EP: I don't mind at all. I'll give you some, some more ammunition…

GG: Okay. I wish you'd give me something tonight.

EP: I got—my mind's going crazy. A lot of things've happened, and everything—crazy. If the kid had called me, I'd probably never have called you back, I guarantee ya…

GG: Who was the fellow that called me?

EP: He's very young—obviously I can't tell you who he is.

GG: But a nice fellow?

EP: He's a very young kid. He's actually a brother of someone—of one of the guys who's with me now.

GG: Well, do you mostly live on the West Coast or Hawaii or…?

EP: Now, don't try to pin me down.

GG: [laugh] Okay, Hawaii. [laugh] That's not pinning you down.

EP: I'll probably be in Washington for…

GG: D.C.?

EP: …for the next several months.

GG: Okay.

EP: But you can't find me…

GG: Oh, okay. I wouldn't know you probably.

EP: If you saw me right now, you'd probably not recognize me. If you looked me right in the eye, you wouldn't recognize me. Anyway, ah, I just got the word, the guy just gave me his hand, I do have to get going, but, ah, it's been a pleasure. I, I hope that people treat you kindly and everything. I'll try to give you some, give you something…

GG: Okay.

EP: …that helps you with different people.

GG: Well, I…

EP: I, I know that they can be very cruel. It's, it's even worse. I thought they were cruel to me when I was a kid, but compared to today, they were nicer back then.

GG: Yeah'll, I know.

EP: They're very cruel.

GG: Well, you may have to help me out, because, ummm, you know, a lot of people are…

EP: Well, don't you worry. I mean, people like you—you'll have the last laugh.

GG: Uh huh. I know, I'm going to…

EP: I can sit back here, but you can sit there and say, well I wish that was true, but see, I can sit back here and say I know it's true until something dramatic happens. I know it's true, but only people, several different people, seem to be very nervous. See, I know what's going to happen.

GG: Well, I'm going to have it…

EP: And I know you're going to have the last laugh.

GG: I'm going to have it written on my tombstone, the words "I told you so!"

EP: Well, I hope you don't die before things happen.

GG: [laugh] Oh, I don't have time to die. I have a lot of ironing to do!

EP: All right, ma'am, it's been very nice talking with you. I, I hope that—good luck with your writing career and everything.

GG: Well, thank you…

EP: You know—come on the bestseller list. You're very talented and ah, you haven't gone through some easy times, but, like I say, you'll have the last laugh. I'll try to call back when things have settled down a little bit.

GG: Okay.

EP: And give you some…

GG: Alrightee…

EP: …see what happens and everything—You are a good fielder, I mean, as far as people. I've seen you on more programs than I can remember. But, I—God bless you, and I pray…

GG: Okay. You too.
EP: God will take care of us all.
GG: That's true.
EP: Whatever, whatever card He deals us, we're going to have to play it.
GG: That's right.
EP: Well, God bless you, ma'am. Have a good night now.
GG: Thank you. Bye bye…

***

(**AUTHOR'S NOTE:** At this point I had not figured out the true reasons for the name change on the grave at Graceland. The caller said I was right about it having been A-R-O-N, but apparently I had the reasons—superstition—for it wrong, I now believe the name change had to do with numerology, as outlined in this book. The caller said he would send me more information—and that he did. And he did call again.)

10

AFTER-DEATH WRITINGS

My examination of the likely circumstances at Graceland on August 16, 1977, has turned up substantial evidence and testimony surrounding the alleged events—and there are undoubtedly many more stories out there yet to probe. I always anticipate finding little pieces here and there to fit into the puzzle bit by bit—however, I am constantly surprised by the curious turns my investigation takes and, from time to time, the powerful new information that comes to light.

Besides a picture taken afterdeath of what appears to be Elvis Presley sitting behind the door to the poolhouse at Graceland, besides after-death taped conversations, besides documented after-death sightings—is it possible that the handwriting of Elvis Presley appears on notes and government documents written after his "death"?

In the late 1980s, I received a confidential telephone call asking me to compare the handwriting on a government document issued by the office of the county medical examiner (of Shelby County, Tennessee) identified as "Report of Investigation by County Medical Examiner" regarding "Elvis Aron Presley."

This is Case No. 77-1944. This report itself—beyond the handwriting that appears on it—raises other interesting questions about the circumstances encountered at Graceland on August 16, 1977.

The medical examiner's report says the body was found "unclothed."

All firsthand reports by those who found the body say that Elvis was found on the bathroom floor wearing pajamas, although the color of the pajamas differs. In *Elvis: We Love You Tender* (written by Dee Presley and the Stanleys), it says Elvis was found "wearing a pair of blue cotton pajamas."

The book *Elvis* by Albert Goldman states Elvis was "clothed in pajamas—a yellow top and blue bottoms."

To my knowledge there are no other reports—besides the ME report—that state the body was found "unclothed," which makes one wonder as to who was seen, and what it was they saw or perhaps were told to see?

Another unusual enigma: The book *Elvis: We Love You Tender* describes Elvis as being alone in his bathroom where he "dropped his book, kneeled over onto his face." This book also quotes Ginger Alden (a friend of Elvis) as having opened the bathroom door to find Elvis "sprawled across the floor."

This same sighting appears somewhat different in the Goldman book *Elvis* with regard to Ms. Alden's discovery of the body: "Finally, she opened the door and peeped inside. What she saw was Elvis doubled up, face down on the floor, with his buttocks elevated, in the fetal position. Clearly, he [Elvis] had been sitting in the black leather and chrome chair reading and had toppled forward onto the floor. The book was still lying on the chair."

Question: How could Elvis be both doubled up and sprawled across the floor? How could he have been reading a book, toppled forward, and then that same book be found lying on the chair? In this scenario Elvis would have been reading the book while sitting on it or—having fallen forward with chest pains—would have been meticulous enough to place the fallen book back on the chair while in the throes of a heart attack.

According to the Presley Commission's *The Presley Report*, the following occurred: "Between 2:00 and 2:30 PM Ginger Alden found the body in a kneeling position, with knees almost touching the chin, resting on the forearms bent under him, head down with his face in the carpet. Ginger called down to Al Strada, Elvis's friend/employee who was in the kitchen. Al came upstairs, then called downstairs for Joe Esposito, Elvis's friend and staff manager. Dr. Nichopoulos (Dr. Nick) was called. Joe, realizing a problem with Elvis and also noticing that rigor mortis had set in, called the Fire Department Rescue Unit #6. Joe and others rolled the body over, then Joe started CPR."

Let's keep the above report in mind as we take a look at the book-in-the-chair phenomenon:

Both Albert Goldman in his book *Elvis* and David Stanley in his account say in retrospect that it was *The Shroud of Turin* by Ian Wilson that Elvis had been reading. *The Shroud of Turin* is a book about Jesus and the evolution of Christian theology. However, upon purchasing a copy of this book, I discovered it had not been copyrighted until 1978, a year after Elvis's reported death.

Perhaps these contradictions are not significant in and of themselves, but consider the following regarding the ME report, which clearly states rigor mortis had set in:

Those first on the scene never seemed to notice this condition but instead thought Elvis to be alive. Ginger Alden has also stated that the thought of Elvis being dead never entered her mind. Albert Goldman's *Elvis* describes a scene in which Joe Esposito was again called. When Joe turned Elvis over on his back he heard a "sighing sound," which convinced him that Elvis was still breathing and thus resuscitation was given.

On a rigor-mortised body?

This raises a question as to what condition the body actually was in when Joe entered the scene. Was Elvis conscious or was he "dead enough" for rigor mortis to have set in?

Let's go back to the ME report. It states that the body was indeed rigored but this same ME report also admits resuscitation was attempted. Since rigor mortis is the stiffening of muscle after death occurs, a condition that leads to fixation of the joints, and considering the body was in a kneeled-up position, wouldn't this rigidity have made attempts at resuscitation almost impossible?

A newspaper interview with Charlie Crosby, one of the medics called to Graceland, once again contradicts the ME report. From the Memphis *Press Scimitar*, August 17, 1977: "Crosby said he and his partner, Ulysses Jones Jr. received the call at 2:33 PM. 'When we got the call all we were told was to respond to 3764 Elvis Presley Boulevard, that there was someone having difficulty breathing...'"

Rigor mortis does indeed interfere with breathing.

Reports apparently disagree as to what was now being done for Elvis. Some say tubes went down the throat into the lungs to administer air directly. An intracardiac injection of adrenaline is often administered in circumstances such as those described; the injection is pumped directly into the heart. Also, in such instances, catheters can be run into the arms, through which drugs can be run to increase blood pressure.

Elvis's stepbrother, David Stanley, recalls seeing no injections or catheters.

In life-or-death emergencies, if all else fails, there is the cardioverter, which consists of two powerful electrodes boosted to opposite sides of the heart, sending a jolt of electricity that can resynchronize the electrical impulses of the heart.

That crisis procedure was not attempted. At least not at Graceland.

When Ken Lefolii, journalist for Toronto's *The Windsor Star*, looked at the homicide report, he saw the following:

> OFFENSE REPORT NO. 2793
> **Subject:** Presley, Elvis
> **Offense:** DOA
> The above subject was brought to the Baptist Hospital after being found unconscious in the upstairs bedroom of his home. The subject was transported by fire department ambulance and was DOA at the hospital.
> Homicide and medical examiner did make the scene at the hospital and at 3764 Elvis Presley Blvd.
> **Status:** Pending
> **Reporting Officer:** Sgt. R.E. Millican

Note the above homicide report states the body was found "unconscious." Not dead and rigor mortised—but alive and unconscious. Two major government reports, the ME report and the homicide report, clash drastically on whether Elvis Presley, the most famous entertainer on the planet, was dead or alive.

That same question has been posed by millions of fans ever since.

When Mr. Lefolii asked to see the rest of the report, he was told it was classified "confidential." The net result of Lefolii's account points to a "conspiracy of silence" surrounding the death of Elvis Presley.

Back to the ME report: It states that Elvis was last seen alive at 8:00 AM. Ginger Alden stated she discovered the body around 2:00 PM, which is consistent with the ME report: "Discovery 1400."

According to the ME report it appears that, although the body was discovered at 1400, there is a time lapse of an hour and a half until police were notified at 1530, and another lapse of thirty minutes before the medical examiner was notified at 1600. What does this reported time frame indicate? Does it mean there actually was an hour-and-a-half lapse of time between discovery of body and notification of authorities? Or perhaps the apparent time lags result from procedural errors, such as mistakes made while hurriedly filling out report forms.

The ME report also reads that Elvis was pronounced dead at 1530. If it's true that Elvis was DOA and rigor mortis had set in, why so long in pronouncing him dead? If the truth is that Elvis was found unconscious, then how could rigor mortis have set in so quickly?

The inconsistencies continue.

Note on the ME report that it reads: "Family consent signed for autopsy to be performed at BMH [Baptist Memorial Hospital]."

Since, as is reported, the only family at Graceland was Elvis's father and Elvis's nine-year-old daughter Lisa and, since Vernon chose not to go to the hospital with Elvis in the ambulance, then we can assume Elvis was not found unconscious or having difficulty breathing—but was already "dead." I doubt Vernon would have consented to an autopsy on a body that was merely unconscious or having difficulty breathing, or was undergoing CPR. Further, as syndicated newspaper columnist James Bacon pointed out, when a body is found unattended, an autopsy is automatic and family consent is not required. Thus why was family consent both sought and given in this instance?

When the ABC network tried to obtain a copy of the autopsy report a Memphis court ruled that, since the autopsy was requested by the family and not the county, the report "was protected by the privacy rule for fifty years."

Someone did not want the public to have access to this information—that party would be someone with knowledge of this medical loophole. Would Vernon, a man suffering from heart problems, a man supposedly distraught over the sudden death of his only son, be so together and in charge (let alone knowledgeable) that he—on the spur of the moment—could even contemplate this legal protection? Even if Vernon was already aware of this recourse, why would it be such an important protection to consider?

What information was there in the autopsy report on Elvis Presley that had to be hidden from the public for fifty years?

Is it not reasonable to assume that this family member who signed consent for the autopsy must have known beforehand about this legal "out"? Remember, the body was reportedly autopsied immediately. Priscilla has said she was in California at the time, and Lisa was only nine years old; it would have had to have been Vernon who signed the autopsy consent papers on behalf of the deceased's family. Odd that this rather simple man was so legally informed at the time of his son's death. Odder still that Vernon was not even at the hospital when the pronouncement of death was made and the autopsy performed.

During an hour-long *20/20* television program (shown in 1979) about the cover-up surrounding the death of Elvis Presley, ABC's investigative reporter Geraldo Rivera pointed out that the contents of Elvis's stomach had been destroyed before the autopsy and that the police had closed the case the night of the death. There are those who argue the reason autopsy remains were destroyed and the report sealed is that the family did not want the world to know that Elvis misused drugs; the argument further runs that the Presley family had enough clout to entice government authorities (such as the medical examiner) to put their jobs on the line and follow through with officially backed concealment of documents usually made public information.

This rationale doesn't make much sense, since the book *Elvis: What Happened?* (written by Red West, Sonny West, and Dave Hebler, who were among Elvis's closest friends) was about to be released—a book that contained page after page filled with stories of Elvis's alleged misuse of drugs. To plan an elaborate cover-up for an image that was about to be smeared publicly seems to be a case of locking the barn door after the horse has been stolen.

Still, there were many in the media who believed that this cover-up was instituted exactly for that reason. Taking a further look into *20/20*'s inquiry into the cover-up surrounding the death of Elvis Presley, Geraldo Rivera ended the hour-long show with the statement that it was the worst medical investigation ever made in this century and that no real medical effort was made to determine the cause of the death of Elvis Presley. Among the various items Geraldo pointed out:

- No real police investigation was ever made, and at nine in the evening of the death, before it was medically or scientifically possible to determine why and how Elvis Presley died, the Memphis police considered this case closed.
- Stomach contents were destroyed without ever having been analyzed.
- There was never—ever—a coroner's inquest.
- The Shelby County district attorney was never officially notified to determine if there were any violations of criminal law.
- All the photographs taken at the death scene, all notes from the medical examiner's investigation, and all the toxicology reports allegedly prepared by the medical examiner are missing from the official files.

Officials of the county government believe there has been a cover-up. None of the doctors at BMH would talk to members of the *20/20* investigatory team about the autopsy results, which prompted ABC to sue Shelby County medical examiner Dr. Jerry Francisco, and Shelby County itself. During the proceedings it was revealed that "no gross evidence of a heart attack or an irregularity in heartbeat was apparent enough to cause death."

Another popular question has been: Why did Dr. Francisco list on the ME report the cause of death was "HCVD associated with ASHD"? HCVD is defined as hypertensive coronary vascular disease, which is a rise in blood pressure related to conditions of the heart and vascular system. ASHD is defined as arterial sclerotic heart disease, which in simple terms means arteriosclerosis, a condition more prevalent among older individuals than younger individuals.

Consider the activities of Elvis Presley: karate, racquetball, and demanding concert tours. It is difficult to believe Elvis could do these activities in such a compromised physical condition, especially since Elvis had had a recent physical, which he passed. However, it is interesting to note that Vernon Presley's heart condition was listed ASHD/HCVD, a condition both father and son were aware of—knowledge that might come in handy if Elvis himself filled out the ME report, the possibility of which leads to the following:

In the late 1980s I received another strange telephone call suggesting that I compare the handwriting on the ME report with Elvis's handwriting, such as the 1979 letter written to President Nixon (reproduced fully in this book).

"You will find the handwriting is one and the same," I was told. I contacted Mr. Paul Weast, a forensic document examiner and master certified graphoanalyst, who is court-qualified as an expert. Weast's report concludes that the handwriting on the ME report is that of Elvis Presley. (This report, in its original condition, is reproduced in this book.)

Study the Weast report and the ME report, and realize that, if you reach the conclusion the Weast report is correct, this means Elvis Aron Presley did not die on August 16, 1977.

Then who did die?

Whose body was found kneeled up on a floor in the upstairs bathroom at Graceland?

***

Why this elaborate, well-planned hoax? If the circumstances surrounding events of August 16, 1977, at Graceland are part of a cover-up and/or hoax, such a ruse might possibly have engaged the cooperation of government officials at least to the point of concealing, or falsifying or altering documents—yet it was a hoax orchestrated to protect these same officials from prosecution.

11

ENIGMAS

Yes, as I proceed in my research, I continue to encounter ever more clues and enigmas. The field of handwriting analysis encompasses many distinct and sometimes clashing points of view—as does any discipline that must constantly come under the spotlight during courtroom testimony. Knowing that courts of law are filled with opposing experts, each challenging the other, Paul Weast believes he can meet such opposition headon with his contention that the ME report filed with Shelby County is in Elvis Presley's handwriting.

"I feel very sure that I will be challenged by other document examiners who will be out to prove me wrong just for their own publicity," Paul Weast wrote me, further stating: "The handwritten 'Elvis Presley Blvd.,' on the ME report is most convincing. The chances that an ME would write 'Elvis Presley' so nearly like Elvis himself writes it are pretty high odds. One letter [another writing sample] does not match exactly, but no one writes exactly the same every time. The slant and size match. That alone is not all that common."

My suggestion is if you the reader have doubts, write the government for copies of everything I obtained, then have these same documents examined by experts of your own choice. If Paul Weast is correct and Elvis filled out his own ME report, then a logical chain of inquiry would be to determine if the government is involved—and, if so, to what degree.

Once again, I think of the words of a mystery caller to my first book publicist regarding *Is Elvis Alive?*: "Tell Gail that the matter concerning the cover-up is far reaching and involves more power and money than she even realizes…"

By the time I began perusing as many government files on Elvis Presley as humanly possible—including FBI files—programs such as ABC's *20/20* had already brought the controversies surrounding Elvis's death to the attention of the public on a scale never before seen. I reeled in shock as witness testimonies and expert opinions changed daily, particularly in connection with how Elvis had supposedly died. Elvis's stepbrother Rick says Elvis "suffocated" in the shag carpeting, while stepbrother David, according to syndicated columnist Liz Smith, says it was suicide. Other close friends suggest it was murder. On July 11, 1990, on ABC's *Entertainment Tonight*, the announcement was made that Elvis's doctor (Dr. Nick) said Elvis was murdered—his death a result of a fatal karate blow to the neck! Dr. Nick was quoted as stating he should have insisted that X-rays be taken. The camera then switched to Dr. Jerry Francisco, who dealt his own death blow to Dr. Nick's testimony: "X-rays were taken—no broken bones whatsoever."

Elvis's friend Charlie Hodge claimed Elvis died of cancer of the bone marrow. (The cancer rumor makes sense in the context of the interview, focused upon later in this chapter, given by close Elvis friends Marty Lacker and his cousin Billy Smith in late 1996.)

It appeared as though an orchestrated smokescreen had been created. Still, during those moments when the smoke temporarily scattered, what became crystal clear was that important evidence had been lost or misplaced in the growing confusion surrounding the death of Elvis Presley.

I was no longer standing alone in my questions. Shelby County commissioner Vasco Smith attempted to reduce the power of the medical examiner's office (Dr. Jerry Francisco) by going so far as to present a resolution to the county commission that would appoint an independent forensic pathologist in questionable deaths. "There seems to be a shield around Francisco's office," Smith said in a Memphis interview. "The Elvis mystique completely pervades the

Memphis area. If there are individuals who are so concerned with the mystique that they do not care to know the truth, then I feel that somewhere along the way someone has to take it upon himself to see that the truth is brought out."

Since it was the medical examiner who had signed the ME report—a report possibly filled out by Elvis himself—and since it was this same medical examiner who oversaw the autopsy—even to ordering that stomach contents be destroyed prior to autopsy—perhaps focusing upon this government official might be a start in uncovering the truth.

The job of the medical examiner is to ascertain the cause(s) of death, and to determine whether a criminal investigation should be launched. When the deceased is a man with the fame of Elvis Presley—a man known to be the target of death threats and whackos—wouldn't the examination of stomach contents be crucial in determining the possibility of foul play? (For instance death by poison?) Destroying stomach contents before autopsy precludes a valid and thorough autopsy.

One would think that with the media focus on Dr. Francisco and the growing contradictions surrounding the death of Elvis, thoroughness would be a top priority.

Dr. Francisco stated the following in a press release on October 21, 1977: "[Elvis's] autopsy was not ordered by the District Attorney General and thus is not a part of the file of the Medical Examiner."

October 21, 1977, is a date that raises yet another question: If you'll reexamine the ME report signed by Francisco you'll discover the date written as "10/21/77" (October 21, 1977), which is two months and five days after Elvis's death. (This date will have great significance as we examine the role that Elvis played in the FBI's Operation Fountain Pen.)

If Elvis's autopsy is not "part of the file of the ME," then what precisely was the role of Francisco? Was he acting under orders from "higher up?" The autopsy was not ordered by the district attorney general; this would indicate Francisco did not see the death of Elvis Presley as being under the jurisdiction of that office. If the Presley death had been under such jurisdiction, it would require a criminal investigation from the DAG's office, making the entire case a matter of public record.

Furthermore, if Francisco was only acting as a family consultant for the Presleys—as he remarked in another public interview—and was of the opinion that this case was not a case for his own office, he should have retired immediately from the case and allowed Baptist Memorial Hospital officials to handle the matter. When the body was being autopsied at BMH, Francisco did not know the exact causes of death. Therefore, to form an opinion about the relevancy of whether to put this case under investigation when the autopsy was not even completed smacks of incompetence at the very least, and may imply a form of complicity on the part of the office of medical examiner and perhaps other wings of government.

Dr. Jerry Francisco has never been known to be incompetent. Just the opposite.

To repeat: Was Dr. Francisco responding to orders from higher up? I believe this is exactly what happened. First of all, assuming Dr. Francisco was under government orders, it would be necessary for him to maintain tight control over the situation by giving the impression that the Presley case was, until October 21, 1977, under his jurisdiction—at which time he publicly announced that Presley's death was a natural one. No one would be able to dispute these findings, because someone had the foresight to have a family member sign the autopsy form, which placed the findings into confidentiality under the state's private-record act.

Francisco's nonchalant attitude during the autopsy and his refusal to allow pictures to be taken during the autopsy, a normal procedure in Shelby County and elsewhere, certainly suggests that Francisco's mind had been made up pre-autopsy as to cause of death. To believe that Francisco was involved in a cover-up of a drug-related death has more holes than substance. Remember, Elvis's death was apparently too sudden for Francisco to think logically or fast enough to order any of a number of forensic tasks that are routinely performed in instances of the sort encountered at Graceland, August 16, 1977. Among procedural omissions were:

- There were no photographs of the body.
- No fingerprints were taken.
- No dental prints were made.
- There was no analysis of stomach contents.

As I further delved into government files, including the FBI files on Elvis Presley, my conclusion was that Dr. Francisco, rather than having played the role of the incompetent, was in reality another hero in the master plan, and thus became the victim of unwarranted accusations.

Do we have evidence that would prove once and for all that the body autopsied was that of Elvis? The paramedics who arrived at Graceland reported to the press that they did not "recognize the body on the bathroom floor at Graceland as that of Elvis Presley." One of the paramedics was also quoted as saying that Dr. George Nichopoulos was giving the body CPR when they arrived, yet Priscilla Presley's account (in the book *Elvis and Me*, written with Susan Harmon [New York: G.P. Putnam, 1985]) says Dr. Nichopoulos arrived just as the paramedics were leaving. Dr. Nick in one account states that he attempted resuscitation efforts because Elvis's pupils were constricted, indicating life. (Pupils dilate after death.)

How strange that Elvis's doctor described a life condition in a body that the ME report states is rigor-mortised. It's also incomprehensible why Joe Esposito would even think of giving mouth-to-mouth resuscitation to a rigor-mortised body, one that perhaps was blue/purple/black, tongue hanging out, face contorted, eyes red. The book *Elvis: We Love You Tender* describes a conversation between Joe Esposito and a doctor at the hospital: Joe asks how long Elvis was without oxygen, and the doctor replies that it was too long, that even if Elvis lives he'd be like a vegetable—which indicates Elvis was alive when brought in. Yet Joe says he found Elvis in a state of rigor mortis.

I also have correspondence regarding a nurse who was called into the autopsy room at Baptist Memorial Hospital.

I was introduced to a respiratory therapist that used to be employed by the hospital that Elvis was brought to on August 16, 1977. She was working that day. Let me say here that she was very leery of talking with me, and made me promise not to ever mention her name, or the hospital that she is now employed with. She told me that a Code 500 was called. A Code 500 is a code that is called when a patient is either in respiratory or cardiac arrest. She was the respiratory therapist who went to the code. At the time no one knew who he was. After it was over, and she was told who it was, she didn't believe it for a minute. She told me that this person had gray sprinkled through his hair, was of muscular build, weighed approximately 180 to 190 pounds and was very, very dark complected. His face was very blotchy and except for his muscular build was trim. She said that everyone who was involved was asked to sign a paper stating that under no circumstances were they to discuss it with anyone, which she did sign, and has not discussed with anyone other than her immediate family and me. She still does not believe it was him and she says that she ought to know because she was putting the oxygen mask on and controlling the oxygen while CPR and other drugs were being administered. She also said that although some drugs were administered, none were administered that normally are when a person has had a cardiac arrest...

This same letter also states:

Another story that I have came from a fan club president in Indiana. She and her husband went to Memphis the same week that Vernon Presley passed away. At the time they only allowed tourists and fans to go to the Meditation Gardens. When they walked up to Vernon's gravesite, it was covered with green turf with flowers on top. Her husband, being as she described "a very nosy person," stepped over the little chain and out of curiosity picked up the turf and raised it up on one side. They were very surprised to see that there was green grass under there with no signs whatsoever of a grave having been dug. It was smooth and level and he even ran his hand under and down the side and bottom of the ground under the turf. There was no break in the soil nor was it sod. What do you make of that?

(AUTHOR'S RESPONSE: Many of those who live around Graceland and/or those fans who visit Graceland, state they never saw any digging of any graves—ever.)

From what is known, there was an autopsy done on a body. Every organ, every inch of tissue, every sample of fluid was dissected and analyzed by several of the top experts in the country. But was it Elvis Presley's body that was autopsied?

According to at least one news report, "No," says Marty Lacker (longtime friend and best man at Elvis's wedding) and Billy Smith (Elvis's friend and cousin, and member of the Memphis mafia). Billy and his wife Jo lived in a trailer behind the main house at Graceland. They played racquetball with Elvis in the wee hours of the morning of August 16, 1977, about which occasion it was reported that Elvis whacked himself so hard in the leg that there was a knot solid enough to cause him to limp. No such contusion is shown on the ME report.

In a late 1996 interview with England's newspaper *The People*, Marty Lacker and Billy Smith admitted that Elvis was still alive, that he had been spirited out of Graceland in the back of a black camper van the day he reportedly died and simply vanished.

The People interview further reports that Marty and Billy said that Elvis met a terminally ill, cancer-stricken man named Scott, who had come to Graceland begging for help for his wife and children. Elvis agreed to help the man, but then saw this man's impending death as providing a means for Elvis to find a new life. Elvis reportedly explained a plan to fake his death to Marty and Billy. Because Scott had the same blue eyes and jawline as Elvis, Elvis paid for Scott to undergo plastic surgery to become Elvis's double. Lacker and Smith claim they were the ones to deliver brown envelopes stuffed with cash to hotels where dying Scott would collect the money in order to make sure his family was taken care of. As Scott's health deteriorated, Elvis's fear was that if Scott died out of town (as opposed to at Graceland) the plan to make a switch would fall apart.

Marty and Billy state they never knew Scott's full identity. They're quoted as saying that Elvis told them that he wished he could be "someone else living a normal life. I feel so alone, so unhappy. I'm tired of all the pressure."

This interview holds personal interest for me because, back in 1988 when I was a guest on Larry King's TV show, Marty Lacker called in. Marty accused me of exploiting the death of Elvis by even asking such a question as to whether Elvis was alive, leaving the viewing audience with the impression that Marty had seen the body in the coffin. Yet in his own book *Elvis: Portrait of a Friend* (New York: Bantam, 1979), Marty said he had not attended either the viewing or the funeral. At the time, I found this puzzling, because Marty was a close friend of Elvis. *The People* interview of 1996 answers this puzzle: Why attend the viewing and funeral of a close friend who is still very much alive?

(**AUTHOR'S NOTE**: Mr. Lacker recently told a fellow colleague that he was misquoted in *The People* and he believes Elvis is not alive. And thus the controversy goes on and on and on.)

If Elvis is alive, then this elaborate hoax appears to be more than simply the result of a man wanting to escape the pressures of fame. Was this in reality a "Musical Watergate"—a chain of cover-ups and secretive escapades that led to the White House?

Affirmation of such an arrangement began when yet another piece of handwriting surfaced, this from the FBI files on Elvis Presley. One piece of handwriting, dated December 14, 1977, four months after Elvis's date of death, is of particular interest: We note the circled printing, "NAM Frederick Peter Pro." Compare the word NAM with the word NAME on a segment of the last page of Elvis's 1970 letter to President Nixon. Compare the F in "Frederick" with the F in "confidential."

Preliminary handwriting reports show that it is Elvis's notation (circled) on the December 14, 1977, FBI report. Elvis, in his own hand, appears to have made a correction to the report's typewritten "Frederick N. Pro" so that it will read: "Frederick Peter Pro," which is the correct name of Elvis's antagonist.

Again, don't take my word for it. Send for the government copies and have them analyzed by experts of your own.

Who was Frederick Peter Pro? What was he doing to Elvis Presley? Why would their names appear together in a FBI file? And, most importantly, what was Elvis doing with the FBI and why would he be correcting files dated four months after his death?

12

LIFE OR DEATH?

There is no doubt in my mind that Elvis had the type of spirit, patriotism and bravery that, if asked to serve his nation, he would gladly serve. Through the 1992 letter from the Department of the Treasury, Bureau of Alcohol, Tobacco and Firearms in Washington, D.C. we know at least that Elvis provided cover for an agent during the period from 1974 to 1976. I needed a date to start with in my investigation of Elvis's personal contacts and possible involvement in law enforcement or other government matters. As far as obtaining the government files relating to Elvis Presley, I had to start my search somewhere, and 1974 seemed a good date with which to begin.

This is when I discovered the existence of Operation Fountain Pen. Government files are very difficult to read, especially FBI files with their "black-outs." (**AUTHOR'S NOTE:** Individual words or entire passages and pages are blacked out in these reports because they relate to matters still classified for security reasons under the Freedom of Information Act.)

Luc Dionne, now a top TV writer in Canada, joined in. Prior to working in television, Luc had been involved with politics—Luc was formerly a political advisor for the Quebec government—work that included the examination of government files and documents. Luc's expertise and credibility would help unfold for the public the story behind Operation Fountain Pen.

Operation Fountain Pen (or, simply, Pen) deals with a racketeering operation the government was investigating. The case involves racketeers who conned billions of dollars from unsuspecting citizens, Elvis being one of them. The simple fact that Elvis was involved is intriguing. In a larger sense it helps flesh out a more complete historical portrait of this entertainer and in the end may help explain why Elvis might have been forced to fake his own death.

These FBI files were not declassified until 1985, almost eight years after Elvis's death. Over six hundred pages of this file are still classified top security, many of them for national security and foreign policy reasons. That so many pages are still classified leaves us to wonder:

- What was Elvis Presley's involvement in this case?
- Why the continued secrecy?
- What was Elvis doing that we are not allowed to know?
- How would this information affect the security of our nation?

We're talking about an enormous amount of government files encountered in the course of our Pen investigation. These materials include (but are by no means limited to) FBI files, trial transcripts, and White House logs—approximately thirty thousand pieces of paper so far uncovered. The documents relating to this FBI operative are thus too extensive to delve into completely via the focus of this book.

This presentation of Operation Fountain Pen as it pertains to Elvis Presley and the circumstances surrounding his reported death is a quick peek into the last years of Elvis's life—the secret part of it.

Earlier, via TV shows and videos such as *The Elvis Files* (as well as a book of same name), Pen has been mentioned. As a result I've received tons of mail asking: "What was going on between Elvis and the FBI?"

Ironically, Pen began around 1974, the same year that Elvis began to give cover to an undercover agent who posed as a musician in his band. A second irony appears when the Pen files reveal that this FBI investigation continued through 1975, 1976, and 1977. Of most particular note are numerous FBI memos and reports transmitted between the Memphis field office of the FBI and FBI headquarters in Washington, D.C. that stated this case ("the Presley case") would be presented to the Memphis grand jury on or before August 15, 1977.

On August 16, 1977, Elvis Presley was "gone."

Until the moment he "died," Elvis Presley was a chief witness against the major criminal organization that was the subject of the Pen operative—an organization that made no bones about its philosophy. A good witness is a dead witness.

The FBI's undercover investigation focused upon an organization called "the Fraternity"—described by the FBI as being composed of approximately thirty to forty of the world's top racketeers, with some members being connected to powerful mafia bosses, including the notorious Gambino family. One "Fraternity" member was an old partner of reputed New Jersey mafia boss Sam ("the Plumber") DeCalvalcante.

There is no question that many of the members of the Fraternity were gangsters, persons described as "very dangerous men who would stop at nothing to scare their victims from testifying."

Beyond its mere ordinary criminal activities, the Fraternity had victimized countless numbers of people worldwide for sums exceeding three billion dollars. By the time the FBI succeeded in infiltrating the Fraternity in 1976 and 1977, the criminal activity of this organization was at its all-time high.

The two FBI undercover agents who infiltrated this underworld group managed to gain the confidence of one of its top men, Philip Karl Kitzer, with whom they traveled extensively. This gathering of evidence against Fraternity members would be more powerful and more prosecutable if the FBI could convince victims to testify. This was becoming almost impossible, since these same victims knew that to testify meant they might be killed and that the lives of their friends and family would be in danger. Even under the best of circumstances, these witnesses would probably have to enter the government's witness-protection program.

Having been frustrated in their efforts to put a stop to the activities of this criminal organization, the FBI received its first big break in 1976 when Elvis and his father Vernon became victims of the Fraternity in an amount exceeding one million dollars. In May of 1976 Elvis and his father entered into a sophisticated sale-lease agreement with a man named Frederick Peter Pro regarding Elvis's airplane the JetStar. Because Nigel Winfield, Elvis's personal airplane broker, had introduced Elvis and his father to Pro, the Presleys had no reason to be suspicious. Not even Elvis's attorney was suspicious. They were all comfortable with the deal and the deal maker.

Briefly, this sale-lease agreement came about because Elvis was having financial problems: bad investments, high payroll costs, expensive gifts, too many assets to maintain, including four airplanes: a Jet Commander, a Dassault Falcon, a Lockheed JetStar, and a Convair 880 (known as the *Lisa Marie*). Liquidating at least one of these airplanes appeared a good financial move. Nigel Winfield was contacted.

"[Winfield] was a former Marine flier and Elvis thought Nigel was the biggest, greatest thing in the world for a while," D. Beecher Smith, one of Elvis's lawyers, later stated. "And during this period, Elvis thought a lot of Winfield and Mr. Presley had no reason to distrust someone that Nigel Winfield called his friend, and Mr. Winfield introduced Pro to us, and because of Elvis Presley's feeling toward Winfield, [he] accepted that man [Pro] and wanted to give him a chance."

After various negotiations between the Presleys and Pro it was decided that the best way for everyone to profit would be for the Presleys to sell the JetStar to Pro on a sale/lease/sublease repurchase plan that was based on the JetStar's upgrade to meet commercial-aircraft standards.

Pro and another Fraternity member were to borrow a sum of $950,000, which could be used to liquidate the balance of the approximately $612,000 mortgage taken out by the Presleys when the aircraft was originally purchased. The remaining $338,000 would be applied to the upgrading that needed to be done, thereby increasing the JetStar's market value to a million dollars. With this upgrading, Pro and his people could lease the JetStar out on a commercial basis and everyone would make money.

Elvis could also lease the plane back from Pro and his associates on an arrangement that would result in a $1,000-a-month profit. In other words, Elvis would have the use of his plane and make a profit—rather than the use of it and have a debit. Further, since Elvis's JetStar was considered private property at the time of the upgrading and still reserved for Elvis's personal use, the JetStar was not then subject to the regulations applied to commercial aircraft.

Pro realized he could make a substantial profit. He confided to friends that—by trading on the added value of the Presley name—he hoped to turn the JetStar into a shuttle service between major U.S. cities and Las Vegas.

Presley lawyer D. Beecher Smith explained: "The transaction involved the sale of the JetStar to WWP Leasing Group. WWP was to borrow enough money from the Chemical Bank of New York to cover both paying off the present indebtedness on the aircraft, which is over $600,000, and also upgrading this aircraft in order to qualify it for Federal Aviation Regulation 121 Maintenance Program. This upgrading had an estimated cost of $350,000. Upon completion of the upgrading, the plane allegedly would be valued on the open market at approximately $950,000. With WWP purchasing the plane, the contractual agreement was for Elvis Presley to lease the plane back for 84 months at a monthly rental of $16,755. Thereafter, Presley would sublease the plane for $17,755 per month for 84 months to Air Cargo Express. This would result in a $1,000-a-month profit for Presley, and at the end of the seven-year period Presley had the right to buy back the plane for $1.00. However, the contractual agreement would allow Air Cargo to continue another three years, paying a reduced rental of $10,000 per month."

WWP would serve as an intermediary between Pro's group and the Chemical Bank of New York. Robert Caggiano and Raymond Baszner, both members of the Fraternity, were given via their World Aircraft Exchange company the responsibility of supervising the JetStar's upgrade.

Vernon Presley issued two checks, each in the amount of $16,755, to WWP Aircraft Leasing Company in payment for the first and the last month's leasing by Elvis of his own aircraft. In order to do his part, Pro drew three checks payable to Presley, the first two in the amount of $17,755 each, to cover the first and the last of his lease payments, and a third payment in the amount of $40,000 given as a bonus to the Presleys.

With an investment of approximately $75,000, Pro took possession of an airplane valued at over $600,000 and, accompanied by his group, left for Miami on board his new acquisition. No sooner had the aircraft taken off when Pro telephoned another member of the Fraternity with the following:

"Hi, Phil. This is Fred. You're not going to believe it. I pulled it off..."

∗∗∗

For the reader's reference I've included a listing of some of the major players in the Fraternity crime organization as they relate to matters the Federal Bureau of Investigation has termed "the Presley case" and the bureau's undercover operative known as Operation Fountain Pen:

THE FRATERNITY: MAJOR PLAYERS

Nigel Winfield: Former U.S. Marine pilot and Elvis's personal airplane broker.

Frederick Peter Pro: A member of the Fraternity. Described by his associates as being "intellectually pretentious," Pro possessed keen organizational skills. He was found guilty of conspiracy and fraud in the Presley case. Acting as an informant for the FBI, Pro was put into the witness-protection program. After Pro and Fraternity associate Philip Karl Kitzer turned state's evidence, it has so far led to the incarceration of some 150 persons in federal prison. Pro died in 1990.

Philip Karl Kitzer: A major player in the Fraternity. As with Pro, Kitzer was found guilty of conspiracy and fraud in the Presley

case and he, too, was put into the witness-protection program.
Kitzer was released from prison in 1988.

Sam DeCalvalcante: "Sam-the-Plumber," reputed New Jersey mafia boss, was partners with a member of the Fraternity.

Robert Caggiano and **Raymond Baszner:** Members of the Fraternity and owners of World Aircraft Exchange.

★★★

SOURCE: Report, Special Agent, Memphis, FBI to U.S.A. Memphis, 03-01-1977, Frederick N.P. Pro, Elvis A. Presley—Victim, Bureau file 87-16994, p. 5.

13

Dealing with the Devil

lvis must have felt like a man walking naked through a village
of cannibals. Elvis Presley, in his stance as victim of an
organized criminal network, might well be the only man both
willing and able to help the FBI in one of its most dangerous undercover investigations. But would he help? For many people, that's
perhaps the most apparent question to ask of a man known to the
world primarily as an entertainer. And if he would help—why
would he? In this case, one has to remember that Elvis Presley was
already a federal agent-at-large with the DEA. In addition, if Elvis
and his father chose to initiate a civil suit against this band of
criminals in order to recover their lost million dollars, it could place
the FBI's entire undercover operation in jeopardy. Would the
victims, rather than pursue their suit through the civil courts,
instead choose to aid the government investigation and ultimately
testify, in criminal proceedings, for the FBI?

As with any such recruitment process, in this instance the FBI
would have had the duty to tell Elvis just how dangerous the bureau
believed the men under investigation to be. Knowing the life-and-
death situation he would face, that his family and friends would
face—would Elvis Presley, the most revered entertainer on the
planet, help the government bring down this dangerous criminal
organization?

Can you imagine the soul searching that must have occurred
when Elvis and his father realized how dangerous these men were?

This was not a movie scene with fake bullets and fake blood; it was not the cartoon hero donning a cape, intent on saving the world from destruction.

This was for real.

Elvis could say no.

But if he did, could he ever look at the man in the mirror again?

Further, the steps he would be taking required a courage that might go unwitnessed by history—except for a chosen few people, no one else could know the details. After all, if Pen was so dangerous for the FBI agents that the bureau found it critical to surround them with surveillance, how much more dangerous was it for a victim who might testify, especially if this victim represented a threat to the entire worldwide network of the Fraternity?

Elvis Presley had become that threat.

As it happened, from the outset Pro's plan did not run smoothly.

The Chemical Bank of New York refused the contract presented and thus refused the $950,000 loan. Chemical Bank wanted a well-defined contract—that is, an agreement that completely clarified and assigned the responsibilities of each party. The bank drafted a new thirty-page contract, a move that would delay completion of the transaction for at least three weeks. Since Pro had counted upon money from this loan to cover the three checks he had issued to the Presleys, the checks were returned marked "insufficient funds."

Further, WWP had added a clause to the new contract drafted by Chemical Bank stating that WWP was no longer responsible for the authorization of upgrading funds. WWP then convinced Vernon Presley to authorize these disbursements, thus relieving WWP of all legal responsibilities. For "some reason" Vernon agreed—an agreement that on the surface appeared a "grave" mistake. Now handling these funds, Vernon ordered Robert Caggiano to bring him the $338,048.33, representing the balance of the $950,000 Chemical Bank loan. To Vernon's shock, when Caggiano arrived in Memphis with the check, he also presented Vernon with five invoices totaling $341,500, which represented the sums owed to the companies that supposedly performed the upgrading work on the JetStar.

This upgrading work had never been done.

Vernon knew this but "pretended" to be convinced that it was the usual practice in the aviation field to pay in advance for work that would eventually be done.

An obvious question: Vernon was known to be tight with money. Plus the Presleys were cash short. Why would Vernon "pretend" to the point of advancing money for work not done? Was this entire situation a setup from day one, and/or was Elvis (along with, perhaps, Vernon) called to action earlier than the declassified FBI files show? Is this why there are still so many classified files? Could another scenario have taken place? Remember, we're talking about May of 1976 to August of 1977, when it's known that Elvis and his father became connected with Pro and his group. What about the letter from the government clearly stating Elvis had given cover to an agent from 1974 through 1976? Recall also that the FBI began its undercover operation in 1974. Consider this:

· The FBI needs a "victim" to testify against the Fraternity.
· The name Pro appears. As the FBI investigates Pro, the name Nigel Winfield comes into play.
· Winfield and Pro are connected.
· Winfield and Presley are connected.
· Presley is a federal agent-at-large with the DEA.

Upon discovering that Winfield is Presley's airplane broker, is it possible that the FBI began contemplating a setup whereby Presley would become a willing victim of Pro and his group via an innocent introduction by Winfield? The FBI then contacts Elvis privately; Elvis's father Vernon has to be let in on it, as he handles most of the financial transactions having to do with Elvis. Since the operative is in its embryonic stage, the FBI isn't quite sure exactly how far its plans will take them or what role Elvis will play. For starters the FBI assigns an agent to Presley and, so as not to arouse suspicion, this agent becomes a member of Elvis's band.

Possible?

Let's reexamine the government letter that states that although

"Mr. Presley was not actively involved in any of the investigations, his assistance in this regard made it possible for our agent to develop a number of quality investigations" during the period from 1974 through 1976.

Human nature would have it that during these investigative years Elvis Presley certainly knew what was going down. He may have even been apprised of the intricacies of the entire operation as it played itself out. After all, Elvis was known for his curiosity and he also knew that people would tell him things that they'd never tell others, even government agents. After all, he was Elvis Presley.

We know of Elvis's love for law enforcement; we know how he loved to hang out with law enforcers. It would be amazing not to believe that Elvis had many gabfests with this secret agent in his band; Elvis no doubt admired the man. Elvis was known to keep secrets, known to love plots and plans. Remember, too, this was the same Elvis who sneaked off to the White House years earlier. I'm sure this investigation excited Elvis. He may at this point have been involved, but not dangerously so.

The real danger developed after the Presleys began doing business with Pro—and became involved in dealings with the Fraternity.

Let's return to the point where Vernon was presented the invoices for the upgrading not done to the Presley JetStar. The following is a whirlwind scenario of Pro and the Fraternity's organized criminal skulduggery.

In this next sequence we witness Vernon's transactions with Pro and his group (the Fraternity), and follow the path of the Presley money involved. We can see precisely how this same money trail resulted in the Presleys becoming (perhaps willing) victims of Pro and other members of the Fraternity.

After lengthy discussions with Pro's group and his lawyers, Vernon Presley agreed to issue certified checks on the invoices to go to the stipulated corporations. Pro immediately cashed the $17,500 check at Presley's bank and put the money in his briefcase. A second check was made out to Air Cargo Express and Dallas Air Motive. Unknown to Vernon, Dallas Air Motive had not been in operation since 1968 and did not even exist in July 1976. Realizing that it would be impossible for him to cash the check without an endorsement from Dallas Air Motive, Pro suggested that Vernon issue another check bearing Air Cargo Express's name only. The third check was issued to Transworld Industries, Inc., which was owned by Fraternity associate Lawrence Wolfson; the fourth check went to World Aircraft Exchange, owned by Baszner and Caggiano. The last payment was reduced by $78,500 and was intended to cover the three bad checks Pro had given Vernon earlier.

Thus a certified check in the amount of $38,990 was handed to Pro in settlement of Invoice No. 506. Pro and his associates left Memphis with a small treasury in their pockets. The only thing left for them to do now was actually perform the upgrading work for which they had already been well paid.

When Pro's second lease payment on the JetStar came due, he gave Vernon another check that bounced—again returned to Vernon marked insufficient funds. Alleging a delay in the transfer of funds that were coming from Jamaica, Pro apologized to Vernon, assuring him that the money was about to be put in his [Pro's] bank account.

The obvious question: How could this man Pro—who only a week before was worth approximately $90,000—suddenly be having difficulties meeting a $17,500 payment?

A few days later, on July 19, 1976, Vernon received a very strange visit: Pro sent a certain R. Warren on a mission to obtain from Vernon the authorization to replace the WWP Aircraft Leasing Company with AGM Financial Limited. AGM was being incorporated under the laws of the State of Florida at the same time R. Warren, AGM's secretary was knocking at Vernon's door.

Disagreements had arisen between Pro and Hans Achtmann concerning Pro's actions. Achtmann (who presided over WWP) had sensed from the very beginning the nebulous character of the agreement between Pro and the Presleys. Constantly on Pro's back, Achtmann had requested that Pro take out a $950,000 personal insurance policy in order to cover the loan issued by Chemical Bank—just in case something happened to Pro. Before deciding to get rid of Achtmann, Pro took the initiative of replacing WWP

Aircraft as intermediary with AGM Financial Limited. Vernon, however, felt he was unable to authorize the transfer from one company to another, directing R. Warren to his attorneys, who categorically refused Pro's request.

Despite his inability to meet his first two payments on the JetStar, Pro was interested in making a second deal with the Presleys, this one involving the Presleys' Dassault Falcon airplane. A little more than a month had passed since the first deal; the Presley clan still felt that Pro was capable of handling this kind of transaction. For them, it was just a question of time before Pro was able to meet his financial obligations. The same sale/lease/sublease concept used in the first agreement was retained this time; however, because Pro did not want to deal with WWP anymore, he suggested AGM should be responsible for authorizing the disbursement of upgrading money. Amazingly, Vernon began negotiating the terms of the second deal. On July 30, 1976, Pro, Vernon, Winfield, and AGM held a meeting at D. Beecher Smith's office.

The Presley lawyer (who also handled the first deal) took care of the details for the second transaction. The scenario repeated itself: Not having any personal checks with him, Vernon issued two counterchecks. The first was for $52,500, representing the first and last payment to AGM, who immediately cashed it at the Presleys' bank. The second check, in the amount of $6,000, was given to Nigel Winfield as a sales commission. For Pro's part, he gave three checks to Vernon. The first two were in the total amount of $28,915.68—which covered the first and last payment; the third check was in the amount of $40,000—another bonus for the Presleys.

Once again, none of Pro's checks were honored at the bank. Fortunately for the Presleys, AGM was unable to find the necessary funds to finalize the transaction. Accordingly, Presley was obliged to terminate the agreement for breach of contract by AGM Financial. Meanwhile, AGM received a visit from two goons sent by Pro to force him to give back the $52,500 paid to AGM by Vernon Presley.

The Presleys never saw that money again.

As lease payments came due in August and September on the Presley JetStar, D. Beecher Smith sent a notice of default to Pro, stating that Presley would repossess the aircraft if payments were not made immediately. On October 11, 1976, Pro temporarily resolved the problem by sending a telex to Presley's bank from Seven Oak Finance Limited in England:

With regard to Elvis Presley—Air Cargo Express transactions, by the request of Mr. Frederick Pro, Seven Oak Finance, Ltd. has bank confirmation that Air Cargo Express has an account in excess of $500,000 US dollars.

Regards
[signed]
AC Scott-Brown,
Seven Oak Finance Limited.

Pro had just committed one of his biggest mistakes. The telex would become the primary piece of evidence upon which the U.S. attorney's office in Memphis would rely in order to indict several members of this important criminal network. The telex secured Vernon, but it was nevertheless the last known time the Presleys had contact with Pro. On the pretext of leaving the United States to get money so he could cover the numerous rubber checks he had issued, Pro disappeared, which severed all his links with his American companies. By this time Vernon had taken enough. At the end of October the Presleys repossessed the JetStar and took the aircraft back to Memphis.

For the Presleys it was a major catastrophe. Vernon had spent $262,000 to pay the upgrading invoices for the JetStar. He had also paid AGM $52,000 at the beginning of negotiations for the Dassault Falcon—plus the $6,000 commission he had paid Winfield. Moreover, Pro owed Vernon $115,000 for the insufficient-funds checks. From May 1976 to October 1976 the Presleys were taken for $435,000 in cash as well as becoming liable for a $950,000 bank loan. In the end, the financial loss was $1,385,000—a nearly $1.5 million disaster that even Elvis Presley could not afford.

Why did the Presleys continue to deal with these people after having been shown such poor faith from the outset? It makes no sense to lose over a million dollars willingly and knowingly—nor to continue doing business with these racketeers, unless...: Were the Presleys guaranteed that such a tremendous financial loss would be covered by the government in return for their testimony? Remember, these aircraft belonged to Elvis. What advantage was there for him to have bonuses included in the deals—bonuses that would only increase the sale price of the aircraft?

Isn't it more reasonable to assume that if the Presleys were desperately looking for buyers it would be more advantageous for their aircraft to carry the lowest possible sale price? Plus there were many points at which the Presleys could have walked away from these deals—when instead they continued to "deal with the devil."

By the end of October 1976 Elvis had been swindled out of over $1,300,000. It's inconceivable that Elvis would not have known anything about this swindle or that his father would not have informed him, especially when one remembers that it was Elvis himself who was giving cover to an agent as early as 1974.

Under normal conditions, the Presleys might well have initiated a civil suit against Pro, Caggiano, Baszner, Winfield, and Wolfson in order to recover their money as quickly as possible. But they chose not to do so.

Why?

The "official story" is that the Presley lawyers decided, along with other government interventions, to present the case to the FBI. However, by presenting this case to the grand jury for criminal indictment and prosecution, the chance that the Presleys would recover their money was next to nothing. By litigating in a civil court, a recoup of their money would have been easier and far less dangerous. Becoming involved in a criminal proceeding meant the Presleys intended to prove the defendants conspired to defraud them. The defendants might end up in jail, but the Presleys would lose their money—and, since the stakes were so high, perhaps their lives would be in danger.

Logically, this doesn't equate.

The scenario only makes sense if my supposition of an earlier involvement with the FBI on the part of Elvis is true. Perhaps so many government files on Elvis Presley are heavily deleted for reasons of "national interest" because an intelligence investigation was conducted—an investigation that would have included the CIA—covering Pro's military-equipment deals with Asian and Middle Eastern countries, as will be outlined in the Pen book.

What we do know is that, based on the Presley case, the FBI succeeded in putting at least a temporary stop to the activities of the Fraternity crime syndicate.

The FBI had their witness.

They won their case.

And Elvis "lost his life"…as he knew it.

***

SOURCE: Report, Special Agent, Memphis, FBI to U.S.A., Memphis, 03-01-1977, Frederick N.P. Pro, Elvis A. Presley—Victim, Bureau file 87-16994, p. 18.

14

"...And Now the End Is Near"

By November of 1976, Elvis's attorney, D. Beecher Smith II, presented the JetStar deal to the United States Attorney's Office for the Western District of Tennessee. The U.S. attorney's office then contacted Joseph Trimbach, the FBI special agent in charge of Memphis. In an affidavit given after the first trial, Nigel Winfield declared that in 1976 "the Dassault Falcon aircraft had been left with me in Miami by Elvis Presley, and in return for my payment of fuel and crew, I could use it." (This permission was given Winfield so that he could find a potential buyer.)

Frederick Peter Pro would later state that Elvis was involved in these negotiations.

Elvis's knowledge of the JetStar deal was further demonstrated by a "private" meeting with Winfield in February of 1977 in which Elvis lied by saying that his father had gotten the money back from Pro. This may have been a test that Elvis was giving Winfield—one to determine if Winfield and Pro were still in contact with each other. Had Winfield been in contact with Pro he would have known that Elvis was deliberately lying to him, a lie that makes no sense unless we accept that Elvis was more involved in the investigation and eventual prosecution of the criminals than he wanted known.

Since these matters were part of a major criminal case, Elvis had to be aware of the most intricate details of what was going on. By the end of 1976 he had to know his life was in grave danger. As to why so few people knew about this case, the answer may be because Elvis wanted to keep as many family and friends out of harm's way as possible. Another reason for Elvis's secrecy and deception may be that he wanted to low-key the situation.

Finally, there can be little doubt that Elvis knew full well who he was up against. Remember, Elvis was deeply connected with various law-enforcement agencies. He was a federal agent-at-large with the DEA. Obtaining confidential information would not be a problem. Thus it's reasonable to assume that Elvis would have known all there was to know about those who might be after "Agent/Victim/Presley." As one friend stated, "Once you started to confide things in Elvis, you had to tell him everything because sooner or later he'd find out."

Elvis would have badgered the FBI about people such as Pro, Wolfson, and the others. He would have learned that Wolfson had been known to the FBI since the 1960s, when he had been wiretapped because of his partnership with Sam DeCalvalcante, a New Jersey mafia boss. These tapes were frightening in the sense that they made references to "killing people and disposing bodies…"

Keeping Elvis's role low-key would become a still more obvious strategy in light of statements contained in a 1978 FBI report:

> The FBI also focused investigative attention upon the activities of a number of sophisticated international "con men" during the fiscal year. In one such case, thirty-four of the FBI's field division participated in an extensive investigation of a complex series of "advance fee" swindles.
>
> Cooperative efforts on the part of the FBI and authorities in several foreign countries resulted in the conviction of five members of this international multimillion-dollar financial crime ring. Those convicted were charged with multiple violations of the Fraud by Wire and Interstate Transportation of Stolen Property Statutes.

For the FBI this investigation was a huge success. The criminal trials that followed would bring about convictions, each in themselves very interesting, some of which will be fully detailed in the upcoming work on Operation Fountain Pen. However, before this success story reached its conclusion, one very special man would be forever sacrificed.

For the world this sacrifice may now be recognized as far too much a "giving" of any mortal man.

The following is a timeline breakdown of happenings in both the FBI operative and the life of Elvis Presley during the crucial phase leading to events surrounding August 16, 1977, at Graceland. It's a date list that is shocking, revealing, mind-boggling, and humbling. No matter what you may now think of Elvis Presley, the truth is this was/is a very brave man who put his life on the line for his country.

December 1976:

While Elvis was at the Las Vegas Hilton he wrote down a personal and troubled thought, tore the page from his tablet, and threw it away. An aide retrieved the note and, years after Elvis's death, entertainer Wayne Newton read the contents. So moved by the note's obvious cry for help, Newton purchased the note, and with Graceland's permission incorporated it into the song called "The Letter":

> I feel so alone sometimes. The night is quiet for me. I'd love to be able to sleep. I am glad that everyone is gone now. I'll probably not rest. I have no need for all this. Help me, Lord...

December 3, 1976:

While performing in Las Vegas—during the 9:00 PM show—Elvis makes a "funny" statement about not living in Memphis, but in Kalamazoo. Turning toward Charlie Hodge, Elvis laughs nervously.

December 31, 1976:

Around two o'clock in the morning, Elvis Presley receives the first of what would become a series of telephone calls with President

Jimmy Carter. This New Year's Eve call is expected by Elvis. According to Elvis's friend, Larry Geller, Elvis and President Carter talked for about ten minutes, with Elvis's only overheard response being, "Yes, sure, I would be glad to..." Geller stated that after the call was completed Elvis told him the President wanted to appoint Elvis to a special advisory position on the youth of America, the music scene, and "some other projects."

At 5:55 AM, Elvis and his group gather together on the *Lisa Marie*, Elvis's private aircraft. Moments before takeoff the control tower alerts Elvis's pilot that airport authorities have received two separate phone calls warning that bombs had been placed onboard the aircraft, timed to explode after takeoff.

Beginning of 1977:
FBI agents Brennen and Wedick are deeply involved in the undercover phase of Operation Fountain Pen. They have already made a deal with Arman Mucci, a "made guy" with a Cleveland mafia family. FBI authorities are so worried over the security aspects of the investigation that they surround the agents with a surveillance team.

The agents have also been invited to a major gathering at the Shaker House Hotel in Cleveland, where they have an extraordinarily profitable meeting that enables them to learn about major scams underway worldwide. Meanwhile, Frederick Peter Pro has returned to the United States from activities abroad and has formed the Trident Corporation; he's ripping off hundreds of businessmen.

January 1977:
Pro is also involved with Philip Karl Kitzer in several deals around the country. The FBI is now investigating "the Presley case" in Memphis, Tennessee. Tom Ronan and Claude Curtis are the agents assigned to this case. Glen Garland Reid is the assistant U.S. attorney working on the Presley case.

An impressive effort of coordination and constant communication is made by the more than thirty-four FBI field offices as well as FBI headquarters in Washington, D.C. The Presley case is to be the catalyst case used to prosecute Kitzer and Pro. The FBI wants to make sure no field office puts its undercover operation at risk. FBI agents Brennen and Wedick's new relationship with Kitzer enables the FBI to learn more about Pro and Kitzer's affiliations and connections—a trail that, as the agents are to discover, runs throughout a wide web of organized crime.

February 13, 1977:
Shortly before a concert, Elvis Presley receives a visit from Nigel Winfield. Although friends Charlie Hodge, Joe Esposito, and Lamar Fike are present, they are not privy to the meeting between Elvis and Winfield. (What actually went on behind closed doors? According to Winfield's testimony, Elvis made some comments about the JetStar deal, but very little else about the discussion has been revealed.)

February 14, 1977:
Elvis concert—St. Petersburg, Florida: Another serious death threat occurs; the bomb squad is in the auditorium—all gifts to Elvis are intercepted and given to a special police squad.

March 3, 1977:
FBI agents Ronan and Curtis head toward Graceland on a call regarding the JetStar deal. At the same time, D. Beecher Smith II, Elvis's lawyer, has been summoned to draw up a new will for Elvis. Witnessed by Charlie Hodge, Ginger Alden, and Ann Dewey Smith, Elvis signs his name to the document. (Around this time, Elvis begins the process of cashing in paid-up life-insurance policies. He sells his bus as well as some other properties.)

March 4 to March 13, 1977:
Elvis leaves for Hawaii. He takes along almost all his friends and their families. It will be their last vacation together. Although generous with his money, Elvis spends most of his time in his hotel room, then decides it would be better for him to rent a private, out-of-the-way beach house on the far side of the island. Friends comment how strange it is that Elvis won't expose his body and that, no matter what the heat, he is seen wearing sweatsuits, a hat

with its brim turned down, and sunglasses.

Regarding this curious behavior, Larry Geller recalls asking Elvis if there was some reason for this cover-up other than that the beach was open to the public.

March 14 to March 31, 1977:
Philip Karl Kitzer, with the help of seven other individuals, develops a plot to defraud a sum of $5,500,000 from the Louisville Trust Bank of Kentucky. A certain John A. of Marietta, Ohio, presents a $100,000 certificate of deposit issued from Seven Oak Finance Limited to the Louisville Trust Bank. Kitzer and his partner are going to use this collateral guarantee in order to obtain the $5,500,000 loan that would later be used to buy ownership of the Eastern Kentucky Coal Company. The plot is discovered just in time.

In October of 1976, five months before Kitzer's transaction with the Louisville Trust Bank, the FBI had advised most major financial institutions regarding the false financial guarantees issued by Seven Oak Finance Limited and the Mercantile Bank and Trust Company. When authorities of the Louisville Trust Bank realized that the certificate of deposit had been issued by Seven Oak Finance Limited, they refused to grant the loan and immediately contacted the FBI. This case became extremely important for the FBI because, after the initiation of the Presley case, the Louisville Trust Bank case became the second catalyst used to stop the criminal activities of Kitzer and other associates involved in the Fraternity.

April 1, 1977:
Having canceled the end of his tour, Elvis scrambles to leave his hotel and, once in Memphis, security speeds him off to Graceland.

April 2, 1977:
Elvis is admitted to a guarded room at Baptist Memorial Hospital in Memphis, Tennessee. No extensive testing ever takes place. The official reason for this "containment" is "nervous exhaustion." From the hospital Elvis telephones spiritual friend Wanda June Hill and tells her he has purchased the white suit he is to be buried in.

April 1977:
Memphis FBI agents have their hands full with the criminal activities of members of the Fraternity. Sydney P., an associate of Pro in Trident Consortium, is now involved in a plot to defraud the First Tennessee Bank in Memphis for a sum of $3,000,000—again using false and fraudulent financial guarantees. This time the pattern is a little bit different: The first step consists of finding a bank employee who will assist the author of the scam. After being assured of a substantial commission, the employee steals some stationery letterheads from the financial institution—stationery later used to write a letter confirming the existence of secure funds in order to obtain a loan. The employee will also be responsible for confirming the letter's validity when a request is made by the financial institution making the loan.

In the case involving Sydney P., it was on April 20, 1977, that Jim McCullough, a vice president in charge of security for the First Tennessee Bank, received an inquiry regarding a $3,000,000 letter of credit issued from First Tennessee Bank. McCullough advised that the letter of credit was false. He immediately contacted the Memphis FBI office. Corbett E. Hart, Jr. (who later became involved in the Presley case) and David H. Johnson, two special agents with the FBI Memphis field division, were immediately assigned the case.

April 1977:
The FBI begins its interrogation of most of the individuals involved in the Presley JetStar deal. Lawrence Wolfson's testimony was probably the most dramatic. Confessing to FBI agents, Wolfson states: "People the FBI didn't even suspect got something out of the JetStar deal, and if these names became known, there could be physical repercussions taken against other individuals."

One of the most dramatic episodes of this entire undercover operation is undoubtedly the "hit" contract placed by Pro in order to get rid of Arman Mucci, a made member of the Licavoli family in Cleveland. At that time Pro was connected to the Gambino family. The Gambino family wanted to take over a $300-million mortgage company. Pro was going to be used as a front man in order for the Gambino family to take over ownership of the targeted company.

According to one of the FBI agents, the hit contract was canceled when the two families—the Gambino family and the Licavoli family—held a council and put a stop to it in order to keep peace.

Thus the FBI knew that Pro—a man Elvis Presley would testify against—was capable of killing. Pro had become upset over a $100,000 check made out to him by Bernard Baker, a check that been cashed by Mucci, who refused to give the money back to Pro.

How would Pro react now that the Presleys were putting their case into the hands of federal authorities? The most significant revelation of this episode is the man hired for the hit contract, one Melvin Weinberg.

Unknown to Pro, Weinberg (who later became a leading figure in the famous ABSCAM scandal in which six federal legislators were indicted for accepting bribes) was now working as an FBI informant. Weinberg's cooperation with federal authorities came about when he had been caught in a major fraud involving advance fees from various businessmen, one being entertainer Wayne Newton. Although conjectural, it is highly feasible that Presley and Newton may have secretly discussed the very dangerous plight they had in common: being victimized by mobsters who were connected to each other.

· Elvis Presley's victimization began with Frederick Peter Pro.
· Wayne Newton's began with Melvin Weinberg.
· Pro contracts Weinberg as a hit man to kill a made guy in Cleveland.
· Weinberg becomes a secret informant for the FBI.

Is it possible that Wayne Newton knew and/or knows about Operation Fountain Pen in major detail? Besides publicizing the song "The Letter," this connection could help explain some of the strange remarks Newton has made over the years.

"We [Elvis] had been friends for years," Newton said in one interview. "I was one of the few people he came to see perform. It was always a qualified friendship." Newton talked about seeing Elvis for the last time in Las Vegas, where they spent many private hours together, Elvis ending their visit with the remark: "Good-bye, Chief, it's all yours now…"

May 6, 1977:
Elvis tells back-up singer Kathy Westmoreland that, although he looks fat now, he'll look good in his casket.

June 1977:
This is one of the busiest months of Elvis's life. Two separate tours are scheduled. Colonel Parker has already cut a deal with CBS for a live taped concert to be shown on TV in the fall of 1977.

June 13, 1977:
Elvis calls President Jimmy Carter at the White House at 6:10 PM. Call is not completed. At 8:43 PM Elvis again calls the President. Call is not completed.

June 14, 1977:
President Jimmy Carter calls Elvis at Graceland at 5:18 PM. Presley and the President talk for six minutes. Approximately one-half hour later the President is contacted by Peter B. Bensinger, administrator of the DEA, of which Presley is an agent.

Elvis stepbrother David Stanley happened to be present when Elvis received the call from the President. Elvis politely asked David to leave the room, stating: "This is kinda heavy. I better take it alone."

June 15, 1977:
Elvis Presley calls President Jimmy Carter at the White House at 8:45 AM. Call is not completed.

It was U.S. Attorney Michael Cody who via the FBI enabled Elvis to get through to the White House—the same Michael Cody responsible for the prosecution of the Presley case in connection with the FBI's Operation Fountain Pen.

June 1977:
During a concert show Elvis utters strange words from the stage: "And I am, and I was."

June 16, 1977:
Elvis discusses with Larry Geller the paradoxes of life; then Elvis's

mood turns serious and he tells Larry: "...things are part of a master plan and some things cannot be explained, at least not yet."

June 21, 1977:
CBS TV special: Elvis looks heavy and bloated, the worst he's ever appeared. Before going onstage Elvis frowns sadly, then turns to stepbrother Rick Stanley and says: "Know what, Ricky? I may not look too good for my television special tonight, but I'll look good in my coffin."

June 26, 1977:
Elvis appears in Indianapolis, looking radically different from his appearance a few days prior during the CBS TV special. Photos taken during the Indianapolis concert show a much slimmer and stronger man than the one on the TV special.

It was as though Elvis had to look his worst for that last documented TV appearance: Here he appears so padded he cannot bend, whereas in the pictures taken a few days later—wearing the same sundial suit—his clothes hang. In these Indianapolis concert photos Elvis is agile and limber, bending with ease. His face is tanned and slim, while only four days earlier his face was ashen and badly bloated—at which time he told people: "America will see me at my worst..."

One cannot lose fifty pounds in a matter of days.

June 26, 1977:
Elvis has with him in Indianapolis the U.S. Justice Department's black book, issued each year to federal agents. Elvis shows this book to friend Larry Geller—it is a book given only to agents. At this point Elvis is scared and nervous. After dozing off, Elvis begins to mumble in a frightened voice how "they're going to get Lisa, they're going to trap her..."

During this time Elvis states that Lisa will be brought to Graceland and that "many changes are going to be made."

June 29, 1977:
Elvis holds his final concert in Indianapolis, the same city in which

the FBI's Operation Fountain Pen series of investigations originated.

June 26 to August 8, 1977:
Numerous FBI memos and reports are being transmitted between the Memphis FBI field office and FBI headquarters. It is anticipated by the Memphis field office that the Presley case will be presented to the federal grand jury on or before August 15, 1977.

August 14, 1977:
Elvis puts his arms around his stepbrother David Stanley (who is leaving for Nashville) and hugs him hard; then, crying, Elvis, says to David: "I just want to tell you I'll never see you again—I love you very much."

August 14, 1977:
Elvis makes a telephone call to Ellen Foster, a woman whom he calls "Luv" in honor of his mother. (Ellen's uncanny resemblance to Gladys caused Elvis to gift his friend with a ring he had once given his mother, now on display in an Elvis Presley Museum.) Elvis reminds Ellen that today is the anniversary of his mother's death, how much he misses her, then says that he is not going on the planned August 16 tour: "No, I'm not sick—I've never felt better in my life, that all my troubles are ending." He asks that Ellen not question him, that one day he will contact her again, and pleads with her not to tell anyone of their conversation and that he loves her very much.

August 15, 1977:
Elvis puts on his DEA jogging suit; he seems nervous but also happily excited. He suddenly decides to make an emergency visit to his dentist. Throughout the night he is happy; he sings, plays the piano, plays racquetball, makes telephone calls.

August 16, 1977:
Elvis Aron Presley is "no more." He is found lying on his bathroom floor. It is a sudden and unexplainable death.

Vernon Presley gives a radio interview to WHBQ's Sid Leek shortly after Elvis is pronounced dead. Vernon, in a matter-of-fact tone, tells Leek that he had seen his son the night before, that everything seemed fine, that Elvis was in great shape—a little overweight but not as fat as the newspapers made him out to be. Unemotionally, Vernon says, "It's hard to believe Elvis is gone." Later that day he signs a deal with Colonel Tom Parker.

August 18, 1977:
Elvis Presley is buried in a secured mausoleum at Forest Hill Cemetery.

October 2, 1977:
The body of Elvis Presley is quietly removed from Forest Hill Cemetery and placed onto the grounds of the Graceland mansion. Graceland is under tight security.

One of the reasons Vernon gave for the transferral of Elvis's body to Graceland was because of a bodynapping plot. Ironically, one of the men accused of trying to steal Elvis Presley's body from the grave at Forest Hill Cemetry was government informant Ronnie Adkins (also known as Ronnie Tyler), a long-time government informant who has spent many years in the Witness Protection Program. Was this a setup by a government informant so that there would be a "good reason to have Elvis's body moved to Graceland"? Is the real truth that if the Mafia suspected Elvis of *not* being dead they might try and dig up the grave at Forest Hill? To thwart such an attempt, moving the body to the security of Graceland makes sense. Whatever the truth, one truth is known: Ronnie Adkins was a member of the Witness Protection Program. It is also interesting to note that when I had lunch with Elvis's Uncle Vester he told me that Vernon was behind the kidnapping ploy, which was later confirmed by Ronnie Adkins. He said he did it as a favor to Vernon Presley. Although there were arrests, all charges were later dropped. Interesting.

October 13, 1977:
A sealed indictment is presented to the Memphis grand jury charging Frederick Peter Pro, Philip Karl Kitzer, and other

individuals with conspiracy, fraud by wire, interstate transportation of stolen property, and mail fraud.

October 18, 1977:
Philip Karl Kitzer is arrested at the Miami airport on his return from Panama. A few hours later the FBI arrests Frederick Peter Pro.

Dr. Jerry Francisco, Shelby County medical examiner, and Baptist Memorial Hospital hold a meeting with Vernon Presley at Graceland. Later that day Francisco announces that he will hold a press conference on October 21 in order to discuss the cause of Elvis's death.

October 19, 1977:
The Presley case (centering on the JetStar deal) is made public for the first time since Elvis's death. The Convair 880 (the *Lisa Marie*) is back at the Memphis airport. Presley attorney D. Beecher Smith II declines comment when asked whether the government's investigation came at the family's request or if the family had participated.

October 21, 1977:
Dr. Francisco holds the much-anticipated news conference. The timing is perfect as the media's attention is focused on Francisco rather than the JetStar story.

February 11, 1978:
Frederick Peter Pro has disappeared and is now considered a fugitive. (According to rumors, the Gambino family had issued a contract on Pro's life.)

May 18, 1978:
Frederick Peter Pro is arrested by FBI agents in Ontario, California.

August 1978:
Frederick Peter Pro agrees to cooperate with federal authorities. According to FBI agent Brennen, "They were desperately trying to set up the trial date on the same day as Elvis's death anniversary."

August 21, 1978:
The trial begins. Despite a deteriorating physical condition, Vernon Presley testifies under strange circumstances: behind closed doors in front of a video camera.

September 11, 1978:
The first trial is a mistrial.

June 26, 1979:
Vernon Presley dies. The second and final victim/witness of the JetStar deal is "gone."

October 1980:
Frederick Peter Pro is admitted into the witness-protection program after agreeing to turn state's evidence against his former partners.

Philip Karl Kitzer is also admitted into the witness-protection program to make available to the state information stemming from Kitzer's strong connections with organized crime.

May 17, 1982:
The second trial in the Presley case begins.

June 14, 1982:
The Presley case ends with the conviction of the defendants.

***

(**AUTHOR'S NOTE:** David Margolis, Chief of the Organized Crime Section of the Department of Justice in Washington, D.C. hung a poster of Elvis Aron Presley on his wall.)

Elvis Presley, for his part, and unlike the criminal defendants in this case, would not have to be admitted into the FBI's witness-protection program. Elvis Presley, a credentialed agent-at-large with the Drug Enforcement Administration, was eligible for the DEA's own agent-protection program.

15
"It's Over..."

Sadly, no one individual, even if he be Elvis Presley, nor an organization as wide and powerful as the FBI or the U.S. government, can totally win its war against crime. Perhaps war itself would end if the dead could return.

If Elvis Presley is alive—and I believe that possibility to be very strong—he must question what difference his role made regarding the fates of the members of the Fraternity. Was Elvis's sacrifice worth it?

Think of how Elvis must feel when reading so many untruths about himself. This must strike deeply into the core of his soul, especially considering what he did in order to make our world safer. His taking a single step into law enforcement had turned into a journey of a thousand leagues.

Did Elvis wonder if those who loved him would forget him? Would his fans understand the truth—that he had not left them but had instead chosen to save lives? The lives of his family and friends—and his own life. For, after all, his enemies couldn't kill a "dead man," could they?

Even if Elvis Presley did die on August 16, 1977, what he accomplished regarding the JetStar deal and the fight against organized crime needed telling. It's difficult not to become overly persuasive in trying to convince the world of something that is "unbelievable." Will telling this story once again place me in the position of being a target of those who say: "Let's kill the messenger who brings the news"?

Should I, like Kelly Burgess, have pulled away from writing this story the moment I discovered the dangerous people Elvis was pitted against? But if I did pull away, then who would come to this man's defense? Doesn't evil exist because so-called good people do nothing?

Imagine what it's like going through so many government files, trying to reduce to plainspoken words an understanding of what has proved to be an increasingly complicated—not to mention hair-raising—story. In addition to the materials covered earlier in this account, there are other papers worth noting here:

- A stock document regarding Elvis Presley dated March 7, 1992.
- A new social-security card that indicated government affiliation.
- Credit cards used by John/Jon Burrows, billed to Graceland.

And what about those FBI files on this case (over 600 pages) still classified top security? My educated guess is that these files remain highly classified because Elvis is alive and may still be helping the government in various ways. (We've just discovered that there are current files on Elvis up to the date of the writing of this book, documents which we've sent for.)

Elvis hinted many times that he was involved in a "master plan." Perhaps because of other considerations—the desire for rest, the desire to study spirituality, and the desire to improve his health and have freedom—he saw the demands of his assistance to the FBI as a legitimate way of escaping, even of getting support from the White House. When you follow the chain of events, especially with Elvis being a friend of President Carter, this type of scenario begins to make sense.

Then there are the many clues Elvis left, as well as some curious enigmas that may bear the stamp of Elvis's sense of play. It also appears that Elvis wanted America to see him at his worst during the CBS TV special. Was this because he wanted those who were trying to kill him to see that he was "sick and dying"? Would they have believed otherwise that a forty-two-year-old singer had suddenly dropped dead?

Elvis made another strange comment to his stepbrother David Stanley toward the end, after David remarked that he'd see Elvis in a few days: "No, David, no, you won't see me in a couple of days. The next time I see you, it will be in another time, another place, on a higher plane. David, you won't ever see me again—alive."

There were important clues left by others: Mary Jenkins, Elvis's personal cook, in her book *Elvis: The Way I Knew Him* (Memphis, TN: Riverpark Publishers) reports that around two in the morning of August 16, 1977, Elvis called down on the house phone asking that Mary come upstairs to straighten his bed. When she arrived, the room was quiet and empty. All the television sets were off— which she found strange, since Elvis was known to keep a television on at all times. Thinking Elvis was in the bathroom, Mary changed the bed, then took Elvis's water bottle to Lisa's bedroom in order to fill it in her bathroom. The room was totally dark, so Mary flipped on the switch. She stepped back, startled: Elvis and Ginger Alden were sitting on the side of Lisa's bed in the darkened room, whispering. Mary said it was all so strange, so unlike Elvis.

Where was Lisa? Nine years old, two in the morning? Was Lisa elsewhere under protection? Had threats against Elvis and his family escalated to the point at which Lisa was not in her bedroom for security reasons? Being told by the FBI how dangerous these men were (the Fraternity), it's a reasonable assumption that Elvis would be anxious that his young daughter might be kidnapped to keep him and his father from testifying (or worse, perhaps Lisa would be abducted and killed as payback for the Presleys' testimony). Could Mary have been called away from the kitchen and upstairs so Lisa could be "snuck out"? Or something or someone else snuck in? (At the Graceland mansion, there's a back staircase leading from Elvis's bedroom down to the kitchen.)

When we accept that both Elvis and Priscilla were cautious about their only child's security, then the account Priscilla wrote in her book *Elvis and Me* makes no sense at all: Priscilla recounts that upon arriving at Graceland in the wee hours of the morning of August 17 she found Lisa outside riding around in her golf cart. Remember, there were journalists, TV cameras, and thousands of screaming, sobbing fans clamoring at the Graceland gates. Under sane conditions the safety of any nine-year-old at three in the morning would be a matter of prime importance. But this child? Off on her own, alone and unguarded in the open on the grounds of the estate for all the gathered to see.

Priscilla then writes she hugged Lisa and left her outside while she went inside to comfort the grieving family. No child, under most circumstances, would be outside at this hour, especially the daughter of Elvis Presley, who only twelve hours earlier had supposedly died.

Priscilla's story:

- Priscilla says she heard the news around noon in Los Angeles (2:00 PM Memphis time).
- Priscilla says she sent for the plane *Lisa Marie*, which was then in Memphis, to come pick her up in Los Angeles.
- Priscilla says she boarded the *Lisa Marie* at 9:00 PM Los Angeles time (11:00 PM Memphis time—consider an approximate four-hour flight time and you have her arriving in Memphis around 3:00 AM).

In the film adaptation of her book, Priscilla plays the arrival in a way completely opposite from that depicted in the book, showing her arrival to be in broad daylight. Her real-life arrival could not have been the afternoon of August 16, 1977, because Elvis's body was not discovered until two that afternoon and Priscilla was supposedly in California.

Was Priscilla already at the mansion, having perhaps arrived at least the day prior to August 16, 1977? In February 1989, I appeared as a guest on Geraldo Rivera's show with Joe Esposito. Geraldo asked Joe about his initial reaction to the news of Elvis's death. Joe was in Memphis at the time. Joe replied that he was concerned about Lisa and Priscilla at the house.

At the house? We know Lisa was there, but Priscilla in her own words states she was in California. If we consider Priscilla might have already been at the house, we may be able to explain the contradictions in Priscilla's story.

Also in connection with the time frame involved here, Priscilla states in her book that she was on her way to a noon meeting with her sister. Noon in Los Angeles is 2:00 PM Memphis time. Upon arriving for this noon meeting, her sister (Priscilla says) had been frantically trying to reach her to tell her that Joe Esposito had called to say that Elvis was dead.

Yet according to Joe's story, Al Strada was the first called, by Ginger Alden, and was told that Elvis was on the bathroom floor. This was reportedly around 2:00 PM. Al Strada rushes up, tries to revive Elvis, calls down to Joe Esposito. Joe has just arrived from the Howard Johnson Hotel. Joe goes upstairs, sees that Elvis is rigor-mortised, but tries to give mouth-to-mouth anyway. Paramedics are called. Joe, I assume, would continue to work on Elvis until paramedics arrive. Others come into the room—and so it goes. Thus when did Joe have time to call Priscilla prior to Elvis's being pronounced dead? If Priscilla's story is correct about the time frame, then Joe was calling her—to tell her that Elvis was dead—before the body had even been discovered.

Another important clue that might demonstrate an extremely well-orchestrated plot can be found in the FBI file report bearing the number 87-143601-7, dated August 2, 1977, in which the assistant U.S. attorney in Memphis was contacted by the FBI regarding the prosecutive action in the Presley case: "…advised that he is prepared to present these facts to the Federal Grand Jury convening in Memphis on or about August 15, 1977."

That projected convening date was not met. However, on October 19, 1977, the following appeared in *The Commercial Appeal*, Memphis's most important newspaper:

6 ARE NAMED IN FRAUD PLOT AGAINST ELVIS

The JetStar is not the Lisa-Marie, Presley's well known and larger converted Convair 880, which was parked at Memphis International Airport last night. The Lisa-Marie was reported to be in Los Angeles.

Beecher Smith, II, the lawyer handling the Presley estate, said last night the plane named in the indictment was under the family's control. "It's safe and in possession of the Presley family." Smith declined comment when asked whether the government investigation came at the family's request and if the family had participated.

Why had Smith refused to confirm or deny the family's participation in the investigation? And why hadn't this small news item made more of a media splash?

Ironically, something juicier was happening mediawise. The same day that the defendants in the Presley JetStar deal were arrested, Dr. Jerry Francisco announced that a press conference would be held a few days hence. What extraordinary timing. Media attention would now be focused upon Francisco rather than the JetStar deal and Operation Fountain Pen. Thus, while the press was being led in one direction, the FBI could continue to pursue their investigation and conviction of a group of men who did not like live witnesses.

Will we ever know the full story? Perhaps more clues to the complete answer to this riddle lie in what Priscilla Presley and Elvis Presley Enterprises are saying in the film *Finding Graceland* together with what Gene Smith wrote (and told me) in his book—that *only* Elvis Presley (Sivle Yelserp) can conclusively tell us what is to happen. And *when* it is to happen.

As Elvis sang in his concert version of "The Impossible Dream" (by Joe Darion and Mitch Leigh, from the 1965 musical *Man of La Mancha*): "...and the world will be better for this, that one man scorned and covered with scars, still strove with his last ounce of courage to reach the unreachable star."

✶✶✶

I'd like to share with you a poem I wrote about Elvis:

WITHOUT A CHANCE

A shotgun house sat in the snow
The moon was cold and grey—
A woman screamed, a baby cried
As night gave way to day.

"What awful luck," the town folks cried,
"For people poor as they."
Twins were born, one had died,
As the town began to say:
"Poor white trash, what a sin,
Those Presleys in such a stance—
The nerve to bring into this world
A babe without a chance.

He'll never own a suit of clothes
Nor a car to call his own—
And Lord-O-Mercy worse than that
What place will he call home?

Dumped upon this weary world,
Lord only God knows why—
Just another hungry child
The world'll soon deny.

He'll be too weak to journey
Those mountains green and high—
In life's valley chained and hopeless,
Never reaching for the sky.

Always hungry, always needy,
He'll whine that life's gone by—
Another lazy, idle child
Singing little but a sigh.

Pity his load this poor child,
Pained, bewildered and thin—
Nothing important he'll ever do
To justify that crooked grin.

His wistful eyes will never greet
The shrines of men and kings—
He's just a poor nobody,
Pimping a pauper's dreams.

Ah, yes, his future is quite bleak,
His life will have such woes—
Just another unspeakable urchin,
Too many thorns upon his rose.

Poor white trash, what a sin,
Those Presleys in such a stance—
The nerve to bring into this world
A babe without a chance!"

As the town tittered and gossiped
About that Presley son—
They forgot to remember life's gift
Belongs to only One.

Laughing and winking and shaking his head,
All-Wisdom expanding His Glance—
God sprinkled a rain of stars upon
A babe without a chance.

God bless you...

***

The poem "Without a Chance" is from the book *Roses to Elvis: Thoughts & Poems of Love From Fans of Elvis Presley* (Gainesville, GA: Arctio/2 A Group, 1992). For information on how to order this book or any other materials mentioned herein, please send a self-addressed, stamped envelope to:

The Arctic Corporation
P.O. Box 6134
Gainesville, GA 30504

For those interested in obtaining a copy of the poolhouse picture in color (as described in Chapter 8), please send a self-addressed, stamped envelope to the above Arctic address.

April 29, 1999

As we try to figure out *why* the shootings at
Columbine occurred, and perhaps what to do
about it in order that it never happens again, one of
the elements discussed is strange dress and odd
mannerisms that cause youths to become "outcasts"
by their peers.

Although I've been out of school for quite some
time, I too, recall a teenager who was quite strange:
He was a loner, he had an attitude that often
resulted in a sneer, he was rejected by the jocks and
the cliques, even to the point of being called names.
His grades were less than great. Many stayed out of
his way, deliberately avoiding him. Others simply
never even noticed him.

He dressed in all-black.

He was the total epitome of an "outsider."

History has proven his "difference" did not lead
him to a life of violence but of service. However,
the "difference" in *why* he turned out where others
of the same ilk have not, may be because his home
was filled with respect for his country, parental love
and more: a deep spiritual base — a love for all
human life and its Creator.

His name was Elvis Aron Presley.

Gail Giorgio

REFERENCES AND RESOURCES

PRINT AND ELECTRONIC PUBLICATIONS

Anderson, Jack. "Presley Gets Narcotics Bureau Badge" (Washington, D.C.: *Washington Post* column of January 27, 1972).

Benner, Joseph. *The Impersonal Life* (Marina Del Rey, CA: Devorss & Company, 1941). Inspirational favorite of Elvis.

Benson, Bernard. *The Minstrel* (Memphis, TN: Minstrel Publishing, 1976). Essay on the power of music and song; contains commentary on impact of Elvis's career.

Brewer-Giorgio, Gail. *Is Elvis Alive?* (New York: Tudor Publishing, 1988). The best-selling book that started it all.

Brewer-Giorgio, Gail, and Luc Dionne. *Operation Fountain Pen* (manuscript for book-in-progress). Investigative account of one of the FBI's most dangerous undercover operations—one that involved, among others, Elvis Presley himself. *Operation Fountain Pen* covers the full scope of the operative.

Brewer-Giorgio, Gail. *Orion* (New York: Simon & Schuster/Pocket Books, 1981; and New York: Tudor Publishing, 1989). Provocative novel about a world-famous entertainer who abandons his career to seek freedom.

Cheiro's Book of Numbers (New York: Arco Publishing, 1964). A classic work in numerology by one of the most celebrated masters to practice in the field.

Cooper, Morton. *The King* (New York: Bernard Geis, 1967). Novel about a singer named Orlando, called "the King," who becomes a prominent government figure.

Cotten, Lee. *The Elvis Catalog* (New York: Dolphin/Doubleday, 1987). Engaging reference work by a noted Elvis scholar.

Elvis: Dead or Alive? (videotape edition of television show with Bill Bixby) distributed by Good Times. (Show televised in 1991.)

The Elvis Files (documentary video). Producers Video, Inc. (PVI) and Media Home Entertainment.

Fairytale (Derbyshire, U.K.: Heanor Record Center Ltd., 1985). (No author listed.) First published by a German-based company as *Bringes Ans Licht* (the German title means "Bring It to Light" or "Reveal It"); released in England under the title *Fairytale*. Novel about the questionable death of fictional rock star Aaron Wade.

Geller, Larry, with Joel Spector and Patricia Ramanowski. *If I Can Dream: Elvis' Own Story* (New York: Simon & Schuster, 1989). Revealing, personal chronicle from Elvis's friend and spiritual advisor Larry Geller.

Gibran, Kahlil. *The Prophet* (New York: Alfred Knopf, 1923). Influential work of poetic spirituality; one of Elvis's favorite books.

Goldman, Albert. *Elvis* (New York: McGraw-Hill, 1981). Enterprising tabloid-style biography of Elvis Presley, written with assistance of Kevin Eggers and Lamar Fike.

Hammontree, Patsy Guy. *Elvis Presley: A Bio-Bibliography* (Westport, CT: Greenwood Press, 1985). Extensively researched work by University of Tennessee English professor.

Jenkins, Mary, and Beth Pease. *Elvis: The Way I Knew Him* (Memphis, TN: Riverpark Publishers). Personal account from Mary Jenkins, Elvis's personal cook.

Kubrick, Stanley (director). *2001: A Space Odyssey* (Metro-Goldwyn-Mayer, 1968; screenplay from a book of the same title by Arthur C. Clarke).

Lacker, Marty, and Patsy and Leslie Smith. *Elvis: Portrait of a Friend* (New York: Bantam, 1979). Personal stories.

Marsh, Dave. *Elvis* (New York: Warner Books, 1982). Biographical account of Elvis Presley.

Presley, Dee, Billy Stanley, Rick Stanley, and David Stanley (as told to Martin Targoff). *Elvis: We Love You Tender* (New York: Dell Publishing Co., 1979). Tales and adventures from persons close to Elvis.

Presley, Priscilla Beaulieu, with Sandra Harmon. *Elvis and Me* (New York: G.P. Putnam, 1985). Memoir from Elvis's wife and Lisa Marie's mom, Priscilla Beaulieu Presley.

Schonfield, Hugh. *The Passover Plot* (New York: Bernard Geis, 1966). Popular novel with plot detailing how Jesus hoaxed his own death. One of Elvis's favorite books.

Scott, Cyril. *The Initiate* (York Beach, ME: Samuel Weiser, Inc., 1920). Spiritual account; among Elvis's favorite works.

Shaver, Sean. *Elvis: Photographing the King* (Kansas City, MO: Timur Publishing, no date). Handsome work from Elvis's official photographer.

Smith, Gene. *Elvis's Man Friday* (Nashville, TN: Light of Day, 1994). Memoir from Elvis's cousin and companion.

Strauss, Richard (composer). *Also Sprach Zarathustra* (1895-1896). Symphonic tone poem inspired by Friedrich Nietzsche's classic philosophical tale *Thus Spoke Zarathustra* (1883-1892).

West, Red, Sonny West, and Dave Hebler (as told to Steve Dunleavy). *Elvis: What Happened?* (New York: Ballantine Books, 1977). Life with Elvis from a trio of former bodyguards and members of the Memphis mafia.

Wilson, Ian. *The Shroud of Turin* (New York: Doubleday & Co., 1978). Historical account of Christian theology and examination of famous shroud held to be that of Christ.

Yogananda, Paramahansa. *Autobiography of a Yogi* (Self-Realization, 1974). Spiritual classic; one of Elvis Presley's favorite works.

ELVIS INFORMATION AND ADDITIONAL RESOURCES

ELVIS IN PRINT BY MARIA COLUMBUS
P.O. Box 1457
Pacifica, CA 94044

All the facts you ever wanted to know about Elvis Presley, in reference format. Write to the above address for information.

THE PRESLEY COMMISSION
P.O. Box 602
Moneta, VA 24121-0602

Write to the Presley Commission for information regarding *The Presley Report* and other Presley Commission publications.

NIXON PRESIDENTIAL MATERIALS
Richard E. McNeill
Archives Specialist
National Archives & Records
Washington, DC 20408

Write the National Archives for information on how to acquire a full set of the Nixon-Presley White House pictures.

FREEDOM OF INFORMATION—PRIVACY ACTS SECTION
Records Management Division/U.S. Department of Justice
Federal Bureau of Investigation
Washington, D.C. 10535
Subject requested: Elvis Aron Presley
Freedom of Information Act (Title 5, U.S. Code, Section 552)

Contact this office for FBI files on Elvis Presley and get copies of your own to peruse.

THE ARCTIC CORPORATION
P.O. Box 6134
Gainesville, GA 30504

Whenever writing for information on materials referred to in this book, please send a self-addressed, stamped envelope.